James W. Skillen

Christians Organizing for Political Service

A Study Guide
Based on the Work of the
Association for Public Justice

Association for Public Justice Education Fund
Box 56348, Washington, D.C. 20011

Printed in Canada.

Published by the Association for Public Justice Education Fund, Box 56348, Washington, D.C. 20011.

First printing, August, 1980
Second printing, January, 1982

Library of Congress Catalogue Card Number: 80-66190

Skillen, James W.
Christians Organizing for Political Service.

Washington, D.C.: Association for Public Justice
Education Fund

113 pages

8009 800313

ISBN: 0-936456-01-9

Cover design by Norm Matheis.

Contents

Preface

The decade of the 1970s revealed that Christians have been re-examining their political lives and loyalties in ways that may change the political landscape of America. Although answers to the question may differ, Christians are asking, "What does being a Christian mean for my political life today?" New groups and movements have arisen, including the Evangelicals for Social Action, Sojourners, the Christian Voice, and the Association for Public Justice. Dozens of books and some new magazines have been published in the last ten years. An increasing amount of press coverage is being given to religion and politics.

After a decade of development and growth, the Association for Public Justice is moving into a new stage of political service in the 1980s. The structure and purpose of the Association need to be described; the work that it has already accomplished needs to be summarized; its general direction and plans for the future need to be set forth. The APJ Education Fund, whose purpose is to educate citizens and to do research toward the end of strengthening a biblical understanding of political life, decided that it was time to write a study guide based on the work of the Association for Public Justice.

The task of writing this short book was an enjoyable one because it was done *in* community, *for* community, and with communal evaluation and support. Many people contributed to it right from the start. Several groups and many individuals in different parts of the country read and tested the first draft, offering numerous suggestions for improving it. Special thanks should be given to Rockne McCarthy, Joyce Ribbens Campbell, Karen De Vos, Stephen Monsma, Jerry Herbert, and Theodore Plantinga for working over the final draft. They cannot be held responsible for the problems and inadequacies which remain, but their help was indispensable.

James W. Skillen
February, 1980

Introduction

This book is a short essay on Christian political responsibility. It is also a study guide. The purpose is to offer a reasoned argument in support of organized Christian service in the political arena. An individual could read the essay from start to finish without pausing to consider questions at the end of each chapter. Or a group of people could use it for study and discussion.

Both as an essay and as a study guide, the book is designed for adults with a fairly high degree of interest in the relationship between Christian faith and political responsibility. One does not have to be a biblical scholar or a political expert to read the text and to benefit from discussion of it in a group setting. At different points, however, a group might find that the discussion will be enhanced by contributions from advanced students of the Bible and politics. Such persons might be enlisted as members of the group from the start, or they could be invited in as special guests from time to time.

If a group plans to use the book for discussion and study, it might consider one or more of the following suggestions. First, in most cases the group should not be too large. The material is meaty and will require good interchange among the participants. A group of 5-12 persons is probably best, though a qualified teacher should be able to use it profitably in a high school or college classroom.

In the second place, it will be essential for most groups to have a discussion leader who has read the entire book before the group begins its discussions. Being acquainted with members of the group, he or she can help lead them through the chapters and the questions with maximum benefit. One person's knowledge of what comes later in the book can keep a group from spending too much time discussing those matters beforehand. Acquaintance with the whole essay will also make it possible for the leader, at the early stages of discussion, to stress important points which he or she knows are basic to later parts of the book.

In the third place, each chapter concludes with three sections of study aids. A discussion group ought to decide how (if at all) it wants to use these aids so that there is no confusion among the members about the purpose of their meetings. The first section, immediately following the text, is made up of questions which can be discussed simply on the basis of the chapter itself. The second section provides additional questions and suggestions, many of which require preparatory work by one or more individuals prior to the group meeting. The final section at the close of each chapter consists of books and articles that can be used for further study.

1

A Hard Look at the Present Situation

Hopeful signs of political concern

There seem to be two major reasons why many Christians are examining and re-examining their political and social responsibilities today. The first is that they hear the Spirit of God calling them to fulfill the commands of Christ to be peacemakers, ministers of mercy, seekers of righteousness, and servants of both enemies and friends (Matt. 5:1-26, 38-48). The people of God exist to be the light of the world and salt of the earth (Matt. 5:13-16). Jesus made it startlingly clear that following Him would require more than words and religious ceremonies. It would demand acts of justice and mercy to every neighbor (Matt. 7:21-27; 10:42; Luke 10:29-37; John 14:12-17). Christians are recognizing that Christ's claim of authority over the entire life of His people has something to do with the way they behave in political life as well as in every other area of life (Matt. 6:24; 22:36-40; 28:18; John 15:5-6).

The second reason is that Christians, along with millions of other people, are waking up to the critical condition of many aspects of public life. This new awareness or consciousness is due partly, but not solely, to a few recent events—the Vietnam War, Watergate, and the energy crisis. Those events signal a deeper crisis in some of the basic institutions and beliefs of Americans. "Could it be," they are asking, "that America's role in the world is not always on the side of the good? Could it be that the quest for ever-increasing economic progress through the use of more and more non-renewable energy resources is a misguided quest? Could it be that America's political institutions and personalities are not fail-safe?" The search is on for new paths to follow, for new solutions to both old and new problems.

It is encouraging, then, to see that many Christians are coming together for serious discussion and study of these matters. Giving thanks to God for a new opportunity to reflect on His Word in the power of His Spirit, they are asking prayerfully how they might together act more responsibly as reconcilers in this world. Biblical study and prayer are leading to action—political action on behalf of the hungry in the world, on behalf of those who receive no justice in the courts, and on behalf of those whose voices are not heard in public life.

These encouraging signs of life among Christians need strengthening, and that is one of the purposes of this book. Political strength comes from seeing what to do and how to do it. The source of power for that strength comes from God Himself through His Word. In the next chapter we will look at some of the biblical basics, but we want to turn first to a realistic assessment of the present situation.

The depth of the crisis

Occasionally during our lives we think back nostalgically to an earlier period—the "good old days," when life seemed simpler or better. That should *not* be our approach as we come to the contemporary political situation. The problems and uncertainties that we face today are not the result of recent accidents or mistakes that have suddenly sent us sliding downhill. They are not so utterly new and different that we would be justified in assuming (or remembering) that political life was a great deal better 25 or 50 or 100 years ago.

Surely our present economic woes are not as serious as those endured in the great depression. Certainly we are better off today with half the voters choosing not to vote than we were when more than half the population (women and blacks) was not *allowed* to vote.

No, if we are to grasp the enormity of the contemporary problems, we will have to do more than contrast our worst fears of today with what we imagine to have been a more trouble-free era. Instead, we should try to understand how the present difficulties have arisen gradually as a consequence of the human decisions, tendencies, programs, and organized structures of at least the past two or three centuries.

Contemporary economic problems, for example, have only been aggravated by the rapidly rising cost of oil in recent years; that is not the first or fundamental cause of those problems. The American desire for ever-increasing prosperity, which determines and is determined by economic processes oriented toward mass consumption, is a desire with deep roots more than 200 years old. Our persistent problems of unemployment, inflation, stagflation, and recession will not be overcome by some technical adjustments in the money supply, or even by the development of new energy resources, if we do not come to grips with their deeper roots, namely, our centuries-old faith in progress and our consumption-oriented way of life.

Or consider another example—the decline of the political parties, the growth of apathy among citizens, and the multiplication of competitive special interest groups. We should not imagine for a minute that parties never suffered crises before, or that interest groups are a new phenomenon, or that everyone voted with joy and satisfaction prior to World War II. Once again, we must consider the gradual historical process through which our political system has developed since the eighteenth century. The seemingly insoluble problems of today are deeply rooted in a system that displays a long-standing faith in pragmatic problem-solving and a faith in a limited government oriented primarily to the advancement of individual freedom and the protection of private property.

We can look around us today and notice that the protection of some private property rights means the failure to protect public health, the environment, or just wages for some people in the third world. We can observe that all Americans do not share a common public philosophy. We can see that apathy or skepticism on the part of many Americans is related to the very failure of both conservative and liberal pragmatists to solve our problems. We should realize, therefore, that the contemporary crisis is not at a superficial level of "problems to be solved" but exists at the very root of the system within which problems are being handled.

At the same time, we should not overlook certain improvements and advances that have occurred in public life during the past two or three hundred years. We will be able to assess our condition accurately only if we are able to distinguish unjust from just policies and institutional structures. Although we have not overcome racism, slavery has been legally abolished. Although disease and malnutrition still plague millions of Americans, many aspects of public health are greatly improved. Although pollution still ravages our air, our soil, and our water, environmental concerns are at least recognized now by the government.

So we must be careful to ask, "What are the real problems? What are the sources of political crisis? How deep-seated are our difficulties? Can we distinguish clearly between serious and superficial issues?"

Christians are part of the problem

Another direction in which we must turn our attention is toward Christians themselves. The problems of politics do not exist "over there" somewhere, entirely in the hands of non-Christian persons and powers. Millions of American citizens claim to be Christians; Christians helped to lay the foundations of the Republic; thousands of Christians hold public office today; a large percentage of Christians believe that our system is compatible with Christian principles. How, then, can we examine the contemporary conditions of American politics without looking at our own responsibility?

This is a difficult exercise for those of us who are Christians because we would like to think of ourselves as part of the solution rather than as part of the problem. But we should try to face up to our own predicament. Christians, unfortunately, have sometimes been among the most self-interested, biased, racist, and self-righteous groups in America.

Consider, for example, how little there is to distinguish Christians from non-Christians in public life today. Self-confessed believers in Jesus Christ are spread indiscriminately across the spectrum of political affiliations from conservative to socialist, with practically no political identity that is distinctly Christian. Many American Christians believe that Christianity should not be directly mixed with politics. Christian faith, personal spirituality, church affiliation, evangelistic work, and Christian fellowship activities are one thing; secular politics is something else. Politically speaking, conservative Christians have more in common with conservatives who are not Christians than they do with politically liberal or socialist Christians. Moreover, Christians are not the only ones who believe that government officials ought to be fair, honest, and law-abiding. Christians were not alone in fighting slavery or working for social security.

Is it possible that we Christians have accepted and adopted so much of the less-than-Christian, humanistic political options of the last three centuries that we no longer have anything uniquely Christian to offer and are unaware of our own spiritual and political poverty?

One of the fascinating aspects of American political life is the paradoxical fact that some Christians view the American system as essentially Christian, or at least fully compatible with Christianity. Others, however, believe that politics is a secular and even dirty business that is not compatible with full-time Christian service even in America. How shall we resolve that paradox?

Probably the most encompassing and persistent tensions among Protestants during the past 50 years grow out of the so-called liberal-fundamentalist controversy which began early in the century. Unique to America, this theological controversy left most Protestants divided in a way that has kept them from cooperation in politics and has hindered the development of a distinctly Christian social and political vision. Fundamentalists and their heirs have tended to look askance at Christian social activism and have been most cautious about mixing or connecting evangelical Christianity with politics, except in certain conservative causes. Theological liberals and their heirs have tended toward social activism of a politically liberal sort and have not always been concerned about demonstrating the biblical basis for their political action. Having given up many biblical "fundamentals" and a strong sense of God's transcendence, many theological liberals have become entirely immersed in human political and social action that is indistinguishable from non-Christian actions and programs.

It is not surprising, then, that we Christians display as much diversity and confusion in our political life as we do in our ecclesiastical life. Before we propose solutions for today's problems, we must face up to our own critical condition as believers who claim Christ as Lord but who show very little unity in life.

Faith + politics = the wrong approach

If there is anything that seems clear in the Scriptures, it is that God claims total allegiance from His people because He is their only Master and the Lord of the entire creation. The Old Covenant with Israel displayed God's complete sovereignty over the entire life of His people. The central command was to serve God only and fully. The New Testament reveals Jesus Christ as Lord God in the flesh—the one who has the right to all authority, who reiterates the Old Covenant's structure of divine sovereignty, and who explains to His people that they can do *nothing* apart from Him.

There is ample evidence throughout history and in our contemporary situation, however, to indicate that we Christians have not adequately understood or practiced the biblical way of life. We acknowledge that we cannot enter heaven without Christ and that we should not worship other gods as if they are competitors on the same level with the God of Abraham, Isaac, and Jacob. But we seem to be quite comfortable voting, buying and selling, studying chemistry, and fixing our cars as if God has nothing to do with such mundane affairs. We act without a second thought as if we are able to do all kinds of things apart fom Christ.

We have grown up learning that politics is a purely "secular" affair of the people. ("Secular" comes from the Latin word "saeculum," which means "of or pertaining to this world or this age.") Since church and state have been legally separated in America and since the church is concerned with "religion" and the "next life" in "another world," politics must be non-religious, secular, and unrelated to God, religion and revelation.

At the same time, however, Christians cannot escape the pull, the feeling, and the demands of God's total claim over all of life. Consequently, many Christians begin to ask at a certain point in their lives, "Doesn't God have something to do with politics if He is Lord over all? Shouldn't I, as a Christian, be able to see some connection between my faith in God and my political actions?" Motivated by questions such as these that arise from a Christian conscience, Christians have asked again and again about the connection between "faith" and "politics," between Christianity and secular government.

But the power of "secularism" already shows its strong hold on our consciousness in the way we phrase these questions. Political life has been practiced and understood for so long as a "purely secular" affair that it seems to present itself to us as something *independent,* as something with a separate identity and meaning *before* it is connected with "faith" or "religion." Moreover, when we ask about the connection between faith and politics in this fashion, we are also assuming that faith or religion is another *independent* experience or practice which has its own identity and meaning *before* it is connected with politics. But starting with these assumptions will always lead us astray. Adding faith to politics is the wrong approach because it means that we are starting with notions of a limited, boxed-up religion and a separate, independent politics—both of which are unbiblical notions.

Proper Christian faith concerns all of life. It has no limited meaning that can be isolated from the political, agricultural, economic, and artistic lives of Christians and non-Christians. Likewise, politics is never purely secular from a biblical point of view. Nothing in this creation (in this world or this age) has a life and meaning of its own, independent of the Creator's will and purpose. Biblical revelation and political life, Christian faith and human government are intimately connected from the start in God's single creation. It is a mistake to think that we should be trying to connect two experiences which have never been disconnected.

What we must explore in later chapters, then, is the integral character of human life in this world. Political life manifests the faith people have, the gods they serve. And the faith by which people live contains within itself an attitude toward politics. Is it part of our problem as Christians that we have too narrow a faith and too secular a view of politics?

The need of the hour

The great responsibility and opportunity that Christians have today is to develop a political approach, a view of government and political community, that renders true justice to every citizen, both Christian and non-Christian. We have already indicated that this will be a difficult task to accomplish because Christians themselves are divided; we constitute part of the problem. We should expect that movements will continue to rise and fall in which Christians will join themselves to "conservative" and "liberal" viewpoints and causes without demonstrating much that is new or uniquely biblical. But it is precisely the renewing power of the authentic Word of God that we need.

Christians have adopted so many positions and perspectives in the name of Christianity that Christian faith appears to be a threat to political stability, moderation, and tolerance rather than the great contributor to peace, justice, and public trust. We should question, therefore, whether the use made of the Bible and Christianity in political life has been legitimate. And we must continue to ask the same critical question of ourselves.

All of this implies, of course, that Christians must be actively repenting of sin. We must learn how to turn away from our superficial, careless misuse of the Scriptures and move toward an authentic, integral life response to God's claim over us in Christ. We must find out how to repent of our easy accommodation to humanistic conservatism and liberalism in the name of Christianity and make concrete steps toward a new politics that clearly and publicly manifests Christian depth. We must not reject politics by reducing Christianity to something narrowly non-political, nor must we accept politics in a way that reduces Christianity entirely to politics.

The United States is a political system that is crying out for new approaches, new options, and new answers. In economics, culture, education, and many other areas, the old rules and assumptions are giving way. It is almost impossible to imagine that Christians will be able to come with significant contributions to public life unless we find ways to work together. That will take deep study, careful formulation of refined and thorough policy options, and demonstrations of our sincere concern for public justice for all citizens. Politics is a full-time calling for some, an ever present concern of all, and an arena of life that can be approached most responsibly by organized associations and groups. What should we do? Why and how should we do it? Those are our questions in the chapters ahead.

Questions and Suggestions for Discussion

1. What are the signs of political crisis that are most evident to you? Why do you believe they are signs of crisis?
2. What are the most healthy characteristics of political life today? For what reasons do you think so?
3. Why do so many citizens express feelings of disenchantment, dissatisfaction, apathy, or powerlessness with regard to political life?

Additional Suggestions for Group Discussion

4. As a group, try to reach agreement through discussion on two lists of public issues and problems. On one list place the most serious, long-standing, deep-seated problems that you believe will require radical change in our political system or in the general direction of our public policies and lifestyles. On the second list indicate the more superficial or limited or specific issues that might require some change but which do not indicate deep or significant crisis.
5. How would you characterize the attitude of your church toward political life? As you were growing up, what kinds of political discussions (if any) took place in the Christian circles of which you were a part? What is your attitude toward political life? Has it changed at all in recent years? Why?
6. Through discussion try to account for the sources of the views of political life that different members of the group inherited from their Christian backgrounds. What are most significant differences among the variety of Protestant streams? Between Catholics and Protestants?
7. If the traditional distinction between "sacred" and "secular" areas of life is rejected, what are the implications for Christians in fulfilling their political responsibility?
8. What kinds of responses from Christians do you think our present political situation calls for? As a group try

to decide what some of the steps should be for Christians to take today in public life.

9. At this point in the group study and discussion, what are your most serious reservations or questions about "organized" Christian political action? About Christians working together *as Christians* in politics?

For Further Reading

John Hope Franklin, *From Slavery to Freedom: A History of Negro Americans,* fourth edition (New York: Alfred A. Knopf, 1974).

One of the enduring injustices of American life has been public racism which expressed itself in the acceptance of slavery early in the Republic and which now continues in a variety of expressions of post-slavery racism. Franklin's history is one of the best.

Bob Goudzwaard, *Aid for the Overdeveloped West* (Toronto: Wedge Publishing Foundation, 1975).

This small book of penetrating essays examines some of the basic reasons for the economic and spiritual crisis in the West from a Christian perspective. The author looks at overconsumption, the gods of Western materialism, structural problems of the modern business enterprise, and the issue of income distribution.

Bob Goudzwaard, *Capitalism and Progress: A Diagnosis of Western Society,* translated and edited by Josina Van Nuis Zylstra (Toronto: Wedge Publishing Foundation; and Grand Rapids: Eerdmans, 1979).

In this larger volume Goudzwaard provides a superb interpretation of the development of Western economic life, motivated as it has been, in his view, by the ideal of human progress toward greater and greater prosperity through the development of science and technology.

Robert L. Heilbroner, *An Inquiry into the Human Prospect* (New York: Norton and Co., 1974).

A frank and sometimes distressing assessment of Western political, economic, and social life that shows the author's serious doubts about whether the United States and other Western countries will be able to face and solve their problems within the present framework of assumptions with which they are working. Heilbroner is one of the most highly regarded economists and writers in America today.

Seymour Martin Lipset, "Religion and Politics in the American Past and Present," in Lipset's *Revolution and Counter-revolution* (New York: Basic Books, 1968), pp. 246-303.

Lipset is one of the best known political sociologists in American academic circles. He has had a longstanding interest in religion in American politics. This is one of his careful surveys and assessments.

Theodore Lowi, *The End of Liberalism,* second edition (New York: Norton and Co., 1979).

Lowi's critical assessment of the American political system is disturbing to those who believe that the free competition of many private interests is the best pragmatic guarantee of public justice. What we have, says Lowi, is "interest group liberalism" which is less and less able to guarantee the success of good government looking after the public interest.

Rockne McCarthy, "American Civil Religion and Civil Rights," *Vanguard* Magazine (January-February, March, 1976).

One of the best popular analyses of American civil religion from a Christian point of view. McCarthy also has several other scholarly essays on the same subject.

Sidney E. Mead, "The 'Nation with the Soul of a Church,' " in Russell E. Richey and Donald G. Jones, editors, *American Civil Religion* (New York: Harper and Row, 1974), pp. 45-75.

One of the best essays in a book that collects a large number of essays on civil religion. Mead is a penetrating historian who describes the American nation skillfully and clearly in terms of its real roots and "soul." His own viewpoint is essentially that of a Jeffersonian deist and rationalist.

Stephen V. Monsma, *The Unraveling of America* (Downers Grove, Illinois: InterVarsity Press, 1974).

An examination of the American political system by a Christian political scientist who is now a state senator in Michigan. Monsma wants to allow biblical revelation to illuminate the problems and prospects of American politics, both domestic and international.

Reinhold Niebuhr, *The Children of Light and the Children of Darkness* (New York: Scribner's, 1944).

A collection of essays on American democracy by the most influential Protestant political-theological thinker in the United States in the twentieth century. Written at the end of World War II, these essays have an especially valuable historical character.

E. F. Schumacher, *Small Is Beautiful: Economics As If People Mattered* (New York: Harper and Row, 1973).

Schumacher was a British economist whose views became a popular sensation in many parts of the world almost from the first year this book was published. As the title suggests, the volume is a critical evaluation of our Western "big is better" syndrome. There are many extremely valuable insights here into the nature of stewardship and the integrality of life.

Egbert Schuurman, *Reflections on the Technological Society* (Toronto: Wedge Publishing Foundation, 1977).

Brief essays that go right to the heart of technologism and its roots in early modern assumptions about the meaning of life in this world. Schuurman points the way to a Christian view of the proper uses of technology for the stewardly care of people and the rest of the creation.

Ronald J. Sider, *Rich Christians in an Age of Hunger* (Downers Grove, Illinois: InterVarsity Press, 1977).

A well conceived and well written book on the nature of world hunger and what can be done about it from a biblical point of view.

Arthur Simon, *Bread for the World* (New York: Paulist Press; and Grand Rapids: Eerdmans, 1975).

This book not only outlines a crucial problem but it shows one of the hopeful signs of political life among Christians today. Simon is the Director of the organization called "Bread for the World" which works to influence federal and state laws and policies so that hunger can be alleviated.

Cushing Strout, *The New Heavens and New Earth: Political Religion in America* (New York: Harper Torchbooks, 1974).

One of the most thorough historical interpretations of American politics as shaped and influenced by various forms of Christianity, secularized Christianity, and anti-Christian "faiths."

Bernard Zylstra, "Modernity and the American Empire," *International Reformed Bulletin* (First and Second Quarters, 1977), pp. 3-19.

Zylstra presents a very fine, compact summary of the nature of the modern spirit—the nature of secularistic modernity. Against that background he then places America in its world role and self-perception in the period especially since World War II.

2

The Biblical Basics

One Lord, total service

The most basic theme of biblical revelation is that the Creator and Redeemer is one Lord who loves and rules and judges the entire creation and expects total service from His people (Deut. 5 and 6; Luke 10:25-37). Kings, judges and lawmakers are not exempt from God's total rule. Their offices are offices of service to God and neighbor according to the commands of the one and only Lord.

Just as the Lord asks children to obey their parents as part of their obedient service to Him, so citizens are ordered to "render to Caesar the things that are Caesar's," and to "submit to earthly rulers" as one part of their total service to God (Ex. 20:12; Eph. 6:1-3; Luke 12:17; Rom. 13:1). But parents and earthly rulers are not the final authority on earth, nor are parents and governors free from their own obligation to submit to God and to fulfill His commands in their various offices (Acts 5:17-32; John 19:10-11; Rom. 13:3-6; Eph. 6:4-9).

The biblical revelation, therefore, has no place for "secular politics" in the sense of a political life that has nothing to do with God's authority and revelation. Thus, one of the most important questions we must ask is: What is the source of our modern sacred/secular dualism that has led us to separate God's authority and biblical revelation so far from practical politics?

At the same time the Bible does show us distinctions between priestly offices and the offices of kings and judges. The life of total service which God expected from His people in biblical times was not without diversity or distinctions. Parents had special authority in family life; priests and prophets performed distinct religious services; kings and governors held unique public offices; teachers and craftsmen displayed their special, God-given gifts and talents.

Today, in our highly differentiated society, we can learn much from the Bible about legitimate differences between church and state, family and school, business and the arts, even though we cannot find exactly comparable social and historical circumstances in the Scriptures. In fact, one of our major tasks should be to try to understand how history has unfolded during the past 2000 years so that we can make proper judgments about the distinctions that exist in our society. We have already suggested, for example, that the distinction between sacred and secular (implying the autonomous, independent, non-religious character of politics) is a mistaken dualism rooted in an unbiblical faith. On the other hand, we have suggested that biblically rooted faith can accept a differentiated society where family, school, politics, church, and business are relatively free to fulfill their God-given responsibilities.

Making these judgments obviously implies a certain view of history in relation to the biblical demands and allowances. We must not only understand the words and the original settings of the biblical injunctions, we must also interpret those words as they illuminate our present situation almost 2000 years after the Old and New Testament documents were composed.

It is beyond the scope of this book to present such an interpretation of history or to offer a substantial exposition of all the important biblical texts that bear upon political life. The study of some of the books and articles suggested at the conclusion of this chapter can help to provide material and insight for accomplishing that task.

For our purpose it will be sufficient to indicate that there are several strong traditions of biblical interpretation concerning Christianity and politics. Emerging from the Middle Ages and continuing through to the present time, especially in Roman Catholic circles, there is a *hierarchical* view that stresses the church's supreme responsibility under God for the life of this world. In other words, in this view the total service demanded by our one Lord is a service entrusted to God's people primarily through the church, with earthly governments and other mundane offices having "subsidiary" responsibility *under* and *through* the church.

Many in the Calvinistic or Reformed Protestant tradition view God's relationship to politics as a more direct, *non-hierarchical* one. Christ is the Lord of all, and His authority is directly related to families, schools, governments, businesses, and so forth, without hierarchical mediation through church officers. Life is integral under Christ's total Lordship; there is no necessary tension among various earthly offices, all of which are supposed to express our love and service to God and neighbor.

The Lutheran tradition has been closer to Calvinism than to Roman Catholicism with respect to politics, but it has had a less integrated view of social life under Christ's Lordship. For many Lutherans there has been a tension between the Christian's internal, loving obedience to Christ, on the one hand, and the citizen's mandatory obedience to government, on the other hand.

Many who stand in the so-called Anabaptist tradition of Protestantism have felt the Lutheran tension between "law and love" but have been less willing than Lutherans to fill political offices themselves. The sixteenth-century Schleitheim Confession expressed the important distinction between what belongs to Christ and His people and what belongs "outside the perfection of Christ." Government, according to many Anabaptists, is *under* God but *outside* the perfection of Christ. Christians should serve Christ and neighbor in love but should not identify with the external authorities which God rules with His "left hand."

Interpreting Old and New Testaments

Given these different traditions, one should not be surprised to find out that there is no univeral agreement among Christians about the proper meaning of the Old and New Testament texts that bear on political life. Nor is there full agreement about the relationship between the Old and New Testaments. The following comments, then, are intended as a framework for discussion or a "stage setting" for the further discussion of some important biblical texts. (Many biblical texts are mentioned in this chapter and at the end of the chapter, and several should be selected for serious study and discussion in a group setting. It is important to stress, however, that in a discussion, members of the group should try to read books and articles from different Catholic and Protestant traditions in order to obtain a better historical sense of the reasons for their differences.)

In our efforts to understand the Bible we should recognize the manner in which God's commands have come to human beings in their historical settings. From Moses on through David and the Prophets, on through the Gospels and Epistles of the New Testament, God revealed His will regarding public law and public life both by way of specific commands about specific situations and by way of basic norms of justice and equity that should hold for a great variety of situations. For example, God functioned at one point as the King of Israel, giving specific theocratic commands. But in other situations He directed judges, kings, and other rulers to do justice by observing His statutes and commandments. Through prophets, through His Son, and through the apostles, God gave us directives which He expected public office-holders to obey as they made and enforced laws. (See, for example, Deut. 7:1-5; 11:1-7, 18-23; I Sam. 16:1-13; Jer. 21:11-12; 22:13-17; Mic. 3:1-4; Matt. 22:34-46; 23:1-12; Rom. 12:17—13:10; I Cor. 6:1-11; Rev. 5:1-14; 15:1-4.)

At the same time, there is no biblical text which indicates God's general command to His people in all times and places to try to set up a particular "model" of government or political community which would reflect most closely some "eternal form" or "ideal state" which God prefers or desires. The chief reponsibility of God's people was (is) not to try to shape their political lives in this world according to one preordained model of divine preference. There is no indication in the Bible that God's concern is for us to try always and everywhere to build monarchies or democracies or some other type of political community. God's revelation was either a specific directive to His people in a particular circumstance, which could not be generalized into a universal principle, or a normative directive which required human response in freedom and creativity. If we take marriage as an example, we notice that God did not define an "ideal marriage" for each couple to use as a model, but rather commanded husbands and wives to love each other. "Love," in the case of marriage, is a norm which leaves each couple free to develop its love relationship in a great variety of ways such that no two marriages will be exactly the same.

The importance of this observation for political life is that we must pay careful attention to the historical situation in which we find ourselves. It is useless (and not biblical) to study the Davidic monarchy as if that historical monarchy with its specific structure and legislation should be a model for us today. It is a mistake to study the New Testament by focusing on Jesus' ministry (which was largely non-political in the sense that He did not participate in public office) and conclude that Christians should be non-political today. The Old Testament situations have something to say to us, but they cannot function as models. The New Testament, as the final interpreter of the Old Testament, has something to say to us about politics, but Jesus' life or Paul's life cannot be held up as the normative model for political practice unless that is what the New Testament teaches.

Rather, we should study the Old and New Testaments in their integral connection—a connection explained by the Gospels and the Epistles, especially the Letter to the

Hebrews (Matt. 5:17-48; John 7:14-29; 8:31-59; Acts 6:8—7:60; Gal. 3:1-29; 5:1-26; Heb. 8-11). We should study them together, observing how certain norms, or authoritative standards, are enunciated in the context of particular historical circumstances. Then, while we recognize that our historical circumstances are no longer those of the biblical writers, we can nevertheless hear the Word of the Lord come through to us instructing us to do justice to our neighbors. We should attempt to obey the divine norm of justice not by trying to copy David's or Paul's response to his situation but by giving creative shape to our own political lives in a way that will manifest biblically normative justice.

Throughout the rest of the book, whenever we use the word "norm" or "normative," we are using it in this sense. God's Word, God's will, offers us His *norm* or standard of justice; it shows us what is *normative,* what is required by God for our lives.

Political action is human response

The crucial point is that political action—whether obeying a traffic law or exercising the responsibilities of a public office—is human historical action. It has the character of a human response (either positive or negative, good or bad) to the divine *norm* of justice and righteousness. Our freedom to be historically creative and diversified in our response to God's will is a freedom we possess as stewards within the bounds set by God's norms. We are free to pursue justice in a variety of public ways; we *may not* (ought not to) act unjustly. God calls us in Christ, through His Word, to respond as faithful stewards of His grace and love. He restores us to the life of human stewardship to exercise all the gifts and talents which He has given to us, including gifts of wise judgment, insight into justice, and the ability to contribute to just laws. (See Ex. 18:13-27; I Kings 3:3-28; Prov. 21:1-8; Luke 12:41-48; 19:1-27.)

If this is an adequate portrayal of the context and spirit

of the biblical revelation, then there are at least two important implications for us today as we attempt to fulfill our civic responsibilities in a way that is faithful to our only Lord, Jesus Christ.

First, we must constantly act with an attitude of true humility. We should undertake every civic duty, every political action, both individual and communal actions, with the avowed understanding that they are *not* God's will but only our *response* to God's will. We should always act in a prayerful, repentant, and forgiving manner, asking the Lord to show us where we are wrong and to bless our actions if they *conform to* His normative will. But clearly it is God alone who will decide if our actions are faithful and just. We may not claim that our deeds constitute the will of God. Our prayer, even for public political life, should be that our *Father's* will might be done on earth as it is in heaven and that we might know the righteousness of God, being able to walk humbly in justice with Him (Mic. 6:1-8; Matt. 6:8-13).

This attitude of humility will lead us to be modest and self-critical in our claims and stated intentions. No one will see us boasting about our fulfillment of the divine will, only to be able to scoff at us and mock God when we fail. We will be able to avoid arguments and fights about who are God's most righteous public servants. We will be free instead to concentrate on the proper duties belonging to God's servants, namely, to encourage, admonish, reprove, and correct one another so that we can grow together in responsibility and wisdom (Eph. 5:1-21).

Humility also means that we can be free and bold in our public service. Recognizing that we are stewards of the Lord, not gods ourselves, and admitting publicly that our actions and programs are a creative attempt to respond faithfully to God, we can then remain open to others and critical of ourselves without being held up at every little turn with the burden of trying to prove that we already know every detail of God's will.

Being free in the Lord as responsible stewards will also help to keep the attention of both our neighbors and ourselves focused on what is most important. The important thing is for us to discern God's normative will, to meditate on His law day and night, to examine our actions in the light of His revelation. Our discussions and debates ought to be focused on what God has said, on what He has revealed, on the implications of His norms. There is no point in being preoccupied with our actions or arguing about our deeds and responses unless we are gaining communal insight into biblical norms by which we can evaluate our deeds. (See Ps. 119; Eph. 5:17; II Tim. 3:1-17.)

The second implication that flows from this principle of biblical humility concerns our view of history. One of the major reasons why people have a negative attitude toward the mixing of Christianity and politics is because Christians in the past have frequently used governmental power to try to impose "God's will" on a particular society. In the name of Christ the Roman Church governed much of Europe in the Middle Ages; military crusades to the Middle East during the Middle Ages were undertaken by the authority of Christ; religious wars were fought for decades at the time of the Protestant Reformation on the basis of biblical authority; and Puritans came to America to set up a new political order that would reveal the biblical righteousness of the city of God.

Not everything done by these groups was evil and destructive; not everything done was contrary to God's will or anti-normative. But it was certainly the case that an attitude of humility toward, and biblical insight into, politics was underdeveloped because Christians claimed all too often that their deeds were the will of God instead of a humble, frail, human response to the will of God. Since they were convinced that their views and deeds were God's will, they did not continue to subject their actions to the Word of God in humility.

Adopting a proper attitude of humble stewardship will allow us to look at the historical efforts of Christians and non-Christians and to judge them more accurately in the light of the Scriptures. If we can take distance from past errors and from prideful arrogance, it will be easier to offer a more distinctive Christian political response that will claim less for itself but which might be more obedient to biblical mandates.

Evangelism and social action

Another consideration for most of us arises from the fact that we are twentieth-century Americans. A tension between evangelism and social action has become an accepted fact in many Christian circles, especially among Evangelicals. The Scriptures leave no doubt that Christians should go forth in the name of the Lord proclaiming the good news of Christ to those who have not heard it. The Scriptures are not equally emphatic when it comes to politics. There is no New Testament command which instructs Christians to run for public office or to form political organizations. One consequence of this has been that evangelical Christians have concentrated on organizing themselves to perform the clear biblical mandate to preach the gospel but have usually felt no responsibility to organize themselves for Christian political service.

The response, however, manifests a dualism of life to which we referred in the last chapter. The Bible is interpreted as a text about spiritual life that can be preached by word and obeyed by verbal and mental assent. Politics, on the other hand, is viewed as a secular realm of human action quite separate from evangelistic proclamation.

But look closely at the concluding verses of Matthew's Gospel. When Jesus approached His disciples in Galilee after His resurrection, He said first of all that *all authority* had been given to Him in heaven and on earth (28:18). He did not say that He had received authority only over the church or only in heaven. Moreover, the teaching of the apostles and the revelation given to John show that Christ's authority was and is truly universal (Col. 1:16-20; I Tim. 6:12-16; Heb. 1:1-14; I Pet. 4:11; Rev. 1:1-8). That proclamation of universal authority is what Jesus delivered as the foundation stone of His "great commission."

Then He said, "Go and make disciples of all nations, baptizing them in the name of the Father and of the Son and of the Holy Spirit" (28:19). He did not say, "Go and preach the gospel in order to get verbal commitments from people to become Christians and join a church." Christ's command to "make disciples" carries with it the full biblical meaning of training people to become completely "disciplined" as Christ-followers. Becoming disciples of Jesus means learning how to function and behave in every realm of life, all day long, in every relationship and responsibility, as people who serve only one Lord, Father, Son, and Holy Spirit.

It is impossible to separate the preaching of the gospel from the training of disciples who can function maturely in every area of life as God's people. To assume that political responsibility can be left untouched by the discipling process is to assume that Christ's Lordship is unrelated to political life. That is a direct denial of what Jesus explicitly proclaimed at the start, namely, that *all* authority belongs to Him.

Furthermore, the command is not to make disciples of individuals but of all nations. People are communal creatures. Their lives are bound together in habits and routines and disciplines of social life. Much of the modern evangelistic enterprise focuses upon individuals, calling them to make a personal commitment to Christ's Lordship. But Jesus is Lord over all groups and nations and authorities, not simply the ruler of individual hearts. People are nations, clans, families, states, and socially organized groups who should become disciples of the King of kings. Organizing Christians into biblically disciplined servants in public life so that the King's justice can be done is one necessary dimension of obeying the great commission in Matthew 28:18-20.

Finally, we must read verse 20 of chapter 28. Verses 19 and 20 go together as one sentence. Making disciples of all nations is not completed by a formal baptism service. The final clause of the commission is: "teaching them to obey everything I have commanded you." Jesus taught many things to His disciples during His earthly ministry, and He promised to send His Spirit to guide them into all truth. Thus, we have to go on from Matthew 28 to study the rest of the New Testament to see what the apostles taught us to do. Some of that teaching deals directly with political responsibility.

One of the biblical basics, then, is that the proclamation of the good news of Jesus Christ must go hand in hand with the discipling of nations. Social and political actions that are obedient to the true Lord and King are essential components of bearing witness to the nations. Our disciplined, total service to Christ, in political life as in every other dimension of our differentiated lives, is an essential component of our demonstration that we are baptized disciples of Christ.

Politics now and God's coming Kingdom

From the end of the Middle Ages until now, which is the period of the rise of modern states, many have come to think of earthly politics as something quite separate from Christ's authority and almost unrelated to His future Kingdom of perfect peace and righteousness.

But notice carefully the final phrase of Matthew's Gospel. After announcing the reality of His universal authority and instructing His disciples to make obedient disciples of all nations, Jesus offered a final word of comfort and encouragement: "And surely I will be with you always, to the very end of the age."

Christ, the ultimate authority over this world, *will be with His disciples always here and now in this age.* Christ's Kingship is not reserved for another age. All people on earth might not see and understand Christ's present Lordship and might not appreciate or accept His merciful and gracious rule over this world, but there is no excuse for Christ's own disciples, His body, His bride not to understand and accept His Lordship in their political lives here and now.

Jesus will be with us as we grow in discipleship *in this*

age until the very end of the age. Therefore our present political lives, just as our marriages, families, businesses, farms, schools, and every other earthly occupation or relationship, are encompassed by the ruling Lordship of Christ. He promises to guide and direct us so that our obedient deeds will be Kingdom deeds, so that our political witness will be an integral part of our witness to His Kingdom, which will come in its fullness at the end of this age.

Jesus walks among the candlesticks of His gathered people (Rev. 1:8—3:22), admonishing, correcting, and encouraging them in their life in this age so that their faithful obedient deeds will follow after them into the coming fullness of God's Kingdom (Rev. 6:9-11; 7:9-17; 14:13; 20:1-6).

Human politics is not an affair of this age alone; it is not a secularized reality, even though some may try to close it off from Christ's authoritative rule. Instead, politics is one important way of responding to the King who rules both this age and the coming age. It is one of the dimensions of our faithfulness to the Lord. Politics is not something we can escape, or something we merely put up with as we move toward the coming Kingdom. Rather, according to the Bible it is an important dimension of our *present* discipleship before the King. Faithful service to the King through deeds of justice is something that should mark our present service, and, by God's grace, we will be able to carry those deeds right on into the coming Kingdom.

Questions and Suggestions for Discussion

1. How should the fact that Christ is King of the kings of the earth affect our present fulfillment of earthly political offices and responsibilities?
2. If human beings are free as stewards to give historical shape to their political lives in diverse ways, how can we avoid complete relativism when it come to norms of justice and equity?

3. Frequently it is stated that Romans 13 and Revelation 13 present two radically different views of government and power in the New Testament. How can these two authoritative passages be reconciled?
4. Can and should Christians exercise penal and retributive responsibilities in government offices, especially when the issue is war or capital punishment? Does the Bible instruct us on these matters?

Additional Suggestions for Group Discussion

5. Spend some time allowing each person in the group to mention his or her present ideas and assumptions about what the Bible says about justice, government, civic responsibility, and so forth. How do members of the group think the Bible should function in shedding light on contemporary political life?
6. With careful preparation on the part of a discussion leader or various members of the group, select several of the following biblical passages for careful discussion in the group. The preparation should include an attempt to understand the context and framework of the passages selected so that the group can discuss each passage meaningfully in its original setting. After a thorough discussion of a few of the passages, turn to the question what those biblical accounts should do for us today. What is the Lord telling us about our present political situation with its historical background? What can we learn from the biblical passages studied?
   a) On God's Lordship, Kingship, Justice, and Righteousness: Gen. 18:25; Deut. 1:17; 32:4; Job 8:3; 34:12; Ps. 11:7; 97:2; 99:4; Is. 9:6-7; 30:18; 40:13-31; Jer. 12:1; Dan. 4:34-37; Matt. 28:16-20; I John 2:29; Rev. 15:1-4; 17:1-18; 19:11-21.
   b) On God's will to have justice exist among people on earth: Ps. 33:5; Is. 1:17, 27; 3:14-15; 5:2; 61:8; Jer. 9:23-24; 22:15-16; Amos 5:14-15, 24; Mic. 6:8; Zeph. 2:3.
   c) On retribution, the use of force, the human offices of

government. and responsibility to government: Gen. 9:1-7; Ex. 18:13-26; Deut. 1:9-17; 16:18-20; 17:14-20; 19:1-21; 20:1-20; 21:18-23; 24:16; I Sam. 7:15—8:22; Prov. 8:15-16; Is. 45:1-13; John 19:10-11; Rom. 13:1-7; I Pet. 2:13-17; Tit. 3:1.

d) On economic justice. equity, and social harmony: Lev. 25:1-56; Deut. 15:1-18; 22:1-4; 24:10-15, 17-22; James. 5:1-6.

7. The Old Testament is filled with passages that deal with the political offices of God's people—Mosaic laws, Davidic monarchy, decisions of judges, and so forth. The New Testament presents us with Jesus, who seems to turn down every chance to become a significant political figure and who teaches His followers to be loving, forgiving, humble, and obligated to turn the other cheek to their enemies. How can we get perspective and instruction from both Testaments for our present political lives?
8. Many Christians believe that since Christ is coming again to establish His final Kingdom, we do not have to worry much about politics now. In fact, many of them would say that we should not expect much good to come out of human politics now. Can this attitude be supported by the biblical message? If not, why not? Why and how should Christians be politically obedient to the Bible here and now?

For Further Reading

Roland H. Bainton, *Christian Attitudes toward War and Peace: A Historical Survey and Critical Reevaluation* (Nashville: Abingdon Press, 1960).

An excellent survey of the different periods of Christian history with regard to the subject of war and peace. It can be read and understood by anyone with interest in the subject.

osé Miguez Bonino, *Doing Theology in a Revolutionary ituation* (Philadelphia: Fortress Press, 1975).

One of the most important contemporary efforts to reinterpret the Bible in the light of political reality is being made by the so-called "liberation theologians" in Latin America. This is one good example of that effort.

Martin Buber, *Kingship of God,* translated by Richard Scheimann (New York: Harper Torchbooks, 1967).

A scholarly study not suited for popular consumption, but an excellent background exposition of the early period of Israel's life under God's theocratic rule. Buber is a noted Jewish philosopher and student of the Bible who sheds much light on the "political" dimensions of ancient Israel's life as defined originally by God's Kingship.

Richard J. Cassidy, *Jesus, Politics and Society: A Study of Luke's Gospel* (Maryknoll, N.Y.: Orbis Books, 1978).

Cassidy draws on many of the best scholarly studies of Luke's Gospel to draw conclusions about Jesus' approach toward and view of political and social life. This is a careful, cautious study that is very helpful in illuminating some of the background elements of Luke's Gospel. Several of the appendixes are special studies of different historical, economic, and political dimensions of that historical period.

Oscar Cullmann, *The State in the New Testament* (New York: Scribner, 1956).

One of the classic studies of the New Testament from the viewpoint of politics and government.

Albert F. Gedraitis, *Worship and Politics* (Toronto: Wedge Publishing Foundation, 1972).

A stimulating discussion of many New Testament passages in the context of an evaluation of the American Christian habit of separating worship and politics. The author's conclusion is that the Bible will not let us separate the two.

Abraham J. Heschel, *The Prophets: An Introduction* (New York: Harper Torchbooks, 1969).

Heschel is one of the most important Jewish scholars of our day. This penetrating discussion of the Old Testament prophets is extremely illuminating. Especially helpful for discussion purposes is the last chapter, entitled "Justice," pp. 195-220.

Meredith G. Kline, *The Structure of Biblical Authority* (Grand Rapids: Eerdmans, 1972).

An evangelical Old Testament scholar, Kline shows that the authority of the Scriptures is bound up with the convenantal structure of God's relationship with His people. God's Kingship and the legal structure of His covenant with His people, therefore, is very important if we are to understand *how* the Bible is authoritative for us and *how* the Old and New Testaments are related to one another.

Richard Mouw, *Political Evangelism* (Grand Rapids: Eerdmans, 1973).

A small, popularly written book that shows how the evangelistic work of Christ's church is connected with politics and political responsibility. This and/or the following volume by Mouw would be good books for further group discussion.

Mouw, *Politics and the Biblical Drama* (Grand Rapids: Eerdmans, 1976).

Mouw attempts to show how the unfolding biblical drama relates to our political life and attitudes. Among other things, he discusses views of pacifists and others with whom he is not entirely in agreement.

H. Richard Niebuhr, *Christ and Culture* (New York: Scribners, 1951).

This classic work explores the most important historical conceptions of Christians concerning the relationship of Christ to culture. Major categories include Christ against culture, Christ above culture, Christ transforming culture, and others. For students of history and the church, this is one of the best studies of this general relationship.

Herman Ridderbos, *The Coming of the Kingdom* (Nutley, N.J.: Presbyterian and Reformed Publishing Co., 1973).

Though this large book does not deal specifically with politics and government, it is one of the best overviews of the biblical teaching about the Kingdom of God. Many sections of the book provide especially helpful insights into the meaning of God's righteousness and justice, and on that basis it is possible to get a much better understanding of how our present political responsibilities are related to the coming Kingdom.

H. Evan Runner, *Scriptural Religion and Political Task* (Toronto: Wedge Publishing Foundation, 1974).

The material in this volume was first presented as a series of lectures at Christian study conferences, and it retains the informal flavor of those lectures. Though parts will be difficult for the uninitiated reader, the book provides tremendous insight into the nature of integral biblical religion and our present political life. This would be another good book for further group discussion.

Thomas G. Sanders, *Protestant Concepts of Church and State* (Garden City, N.Y.: Doubleday Anchor Books, 1964).

An excellent introduction to the most important traditions of Protestant life and thought regarding political life.

James W. Skillen, "Augustine and Contemporary Evangelical Social Thought," *The Reformed Journal,* (January, 1979), pp. 19-24.

An argument that the basic lines of thought and reasons for controversy among contemporary Protestants (Lutherans, Calvinists, Anabaptists, etc.) are rooted in the structures of thought of St. Augustine, who held several competing views of political life himself.

Herman Veldkamp, *The Farmer from Tekoa: On the Book of Amos*, translated by Theodore Plantinga (St. Catharines, Ontario: Paideia Press, 1977).

A popular exposition of the book of Amos, highlighting the political implications of the prophet's message as addressed to the Old Testament people of God.

Donald J. Wolf, S.J., *Toward Consensus: Catholic-Protestant Interpretations of Church and State* (Garden City, N.Y.: Doubleday Anchor Books, 1968).

A fine study which gives special attention to the American situation, arguing that there is an emerging consensus among Catholics and Protestants on what the proper relationship between church and state should be.

John Howard Yoder, *The Politics of Jesus* (Grand Rapids: Eerdmans, 1972).

One of the best expositions of the New Testament material from an Anabaptist, non-violent point of view. Jesus' life and ministry have radical implications for politics, according to Yoder.

Bernard Zylstra, "The Bible, Justice and the State," *International Reformed Bulletin,* Vol. 16 (Fall, 1973), pp. 2-18.

A superb article from a Reformed Protestant point of view that discusses all three of the subjects mentioned in the title.

3

Justice in the Political Community

Authority in community

Serving the Lord by doing justice in politics requires that we understand the nature of the political community. We are using the phrase "political community" to refer to the "state" or "nation." There is considerable confusion about terms such as "state," "government," "politics," "nation," and "society," and we need to explain what we mean.

In the New Testament writings the primary references to political life are references to the "authorities" who have responsibility to govern, and to the "subjects" who have responsibility to be obedient to the authorities as unto the Lord (John 19:11; Rom. 13:1-7; I Tim. 2:1-2; I Pet. 2:13-14). Though it is not always stated explicitly, the implication is that *both* the "authorities" and the "subjects" are responsible for contributing to a community of peace and justice (I Tim. 2:2; Rom. 13:3).

It is true, however, that most "subjects" in the first century did not have much freedom to do anything except submit to what was required of them by the authorities, even when the authorities were not acting justly. Subjects had no voting rights, no political parties, no highly organized lobby groups. In fact, some of the most courageous and responsible acts by citizens were those of disobedience by Christians who refused to treat the Roman Caesar as God. They demonstrated with great courage that "subjection" to earthly authorities cannot be absolute since even earthly authorities must be *subject* to the authority of Christ.

Today, after centuries of change, part of which has been influenced by the power of Christian dedication to Christ, the dominant political reality in the world is not an emperor in an empire but the modern "state." And in our American *federal state* we have wide opportunities to participate as "citizens"—not merely as "subjects"—in its affairs. Our primary difficulty in the United States is almost the reverse of the one faced by early Christians. After centuries of revolution against authority in the West, people in our day hardly recognize that government should be an office of public authority to which citizens ought to be subject as unto the Lord for the sake of peace and justice. Instead, we tend to view government as nothing more than an extension of the right of citizens to be self-ruling, self-determining, and free from any authority other than themselves.

The fact that we have many participatory rights today should not keep us from recognizing that *citizens* are still *subjects* and that *governments* are still *authorities.* Both citizens and governments have God-given responsibilities to serve the public in their respective offices by doing justice. Moreover, we need to emphasize that the political community of rulers and subjects, of governments and citizens, is a community of mutual responsibility and accountability for public justice. Both the government and the citizens have a common, normative task to subject (submit) themselves to God so that justice and peace can rule in the public community.

For these reasons we prefer to use the phrase "political community" instead of the word "state" to refer to the public reality which includes both citizens and the government. "Political community" emphasizes the reality of a common public trust that all hold in common. The word "state" does not always suggest this idea, and besides, many people confuse "state" with "government."

Government is not the state, but only the proper authority within the political community. Government includes executive, legislative, and judicial branches at all levels—federal, state, and local. Governments at all these levels and in all branches have the responsibility of establishing, enforcing, and adjudicating public laws for the sake of justice for all citizens. Citizens are subject to the governing authorities with the responsibility to obey and with the freedom to help shape just laws and good government. The authorities in the community are subject to God as office-bearers with the responsibility to govern justly.

Access to authority

For centuries many governments have ruled autocratically and arbitrarily without regard to their normative responsibility before God as stewards of justice and without paying sufficient attention to the needs and desires of their subjects. Reaction to that kind of authoritarianism has arisen vigorously and for sustained periods of time from subjected peoples. In the United States we have a political system that is strongly oriented toward the protection of citizens from authoritarian and autocratic governments. The separation and balance of powers, the federal structure, the principle of the rule of law, regular elections, and many other devices are designed to keep power from being concentrated in too few hands that might use it arbitrarily. The assumption is that if citizens are granted *free access* to power through elected representatives, judicial appeals, and other means, then political authority will be held accountable and used responsibly.

Our American problem, however, is that we have placed too much emphasis on the *form* of limited government, and not enough on the *norm* for limited government. We have made sure that no monarch can rule us, but we are not very clear about the norms by which a majority-elected

Congress and President should rule. We have put up barriers against the concentration of power, but we have not done much to clarify the purpose which should guide the authorities that do have limited power. We have sought to avoid subjection to a single autocratic will, but we have not figured out how to avoid subjection to the almost absolute power of the "will of the people." The key assumption throughout U.S. history seems to have been that if citizens have access to authority, they can guarantee their own freedom and good government. But is this true?

The framework of this system is conditioned almost entirely by the idea of a mutual opposition or mistrust between authorities and citizens. It is structured primarily to avoid distortions and abuses of power rather than to obey a divine norm for the public good by strengthening legitimate public authority.

As Christians we should take a different point of departure. Access by citizens to public authority is certainly a legitimate principle for modern political communities. If citizens are to be responsible for obeying laws and promoting peace and justice, then they need some legitimate framework for participation. But participation should be seen as the opportunity to help authorities and fellow citizens fulfill their offices of public responsibility, not merely as the right of citizens to express their wills over against the government's will. A community of public justice cannot be achieved by the competition of self-interests, but only through a common desire to establish normative justice for all.

The primary desire of citizens should not be to have their competitive interests represented but to have different views of public justice represented so that adequate debate can take place about the purpose and limits of the political community. Civic participation is crucial if a public community is going to be a true community. But access to authority can abuse power as easily as it can guide it responsibly, because various interests can gain so much influence over public authorities that the authorities are unable to render true public justice but can only give their backing to particular special interests among the citizens. Unfortunately, this is our condition in the U.S., where interest-group politics frequently (if not always) predominates over the public good. Access to authority should not end up as the triumph of one or more private interests over public authority. It should allow all citizens the opportunity to participate in strengthening legitimate authority and in establishing just public laws that will encourage a willing obedience on the part of citizens who are subject to the authorities.

Public justice is a norm

The norm for life in the political community, then, is public justice. In other words, the controlling principle by which public laws, government decisions, and civic participation ought to be judged is that of public justice. The norm, or guiding principle, is not democratic procedure or majority rule or even equality, but public justice. The reason why most American believe that democracy and majority rule and equality are important is because these political characteristics seem to offer the best possibility for maintaining a *just* public order. That might or might not be the case. Judgment should be made about them on the basis of whether or not they contribute to public justice. By examining the norm of public justice we can expose some of the deficiencies of interest-group politics and also indicate a few of the defining elements of the political community.

The norm of public justice implies the existence of a public realm, a public community to which we belong as citizens. The norm of justice holds for that realm. The crucial question that should occupy us is: "What is a just public community?" or "When and how is a political community truly just?" This is quite different from the question "How should we vote?" or "How should we look after our interests in the public realm?" The first concern is not about voting rights or the structure of government or restraints on government. All these matters have to be determined on the basis of knowing what the political community ought to be, in its basic identity, as it takes shape in accord with justice.

Admittedly, it is difficult to define "public justice" with a simple phrase or two. To say that justice means giving everyone his or her due is not enough, though it is important. "Justice" is a term very much like "beauty" or "goodness." It is almost impossible in a sentence to define what is beautiful about a work of art. But it is certainly no more difficult to understand what public justice is than it is to understand what the "national interest" is. When the President or a member of Congress says that a particular action or law is in the national interest, it is never self-evident what that means. Signing a treaty for nuclear arms control, selling or not selling tons of wheat to other countries, or lowering taxes can each be put forward on the grounds that it serves the national interest. But many might protest that such an action or law is *not* in the national interest. Most people do not agree about what the national interest is, though most believe that the President and Congress should serve the national interest.

From a Christian point of view, public justice rather than national interest ought to serve as the highest political norm. It will, of course, be necessary to debate whether or not a particular action or law might advance or hinder public justice, but we should carry on our debate in search of laws and actions that will promote the universal justice of our public political community and of all countries and peoples.

The primary fault of interest-group politics is that it does not focus attention on public justice. The guiding assumption is that if every group seeks its own interest in competition with others and if the government tries to balance all the interests, the net result will be good for everyone. Our political system emphasizes procedures and processes for carrying on the expression of interests, but it does not emphasize the prior and overruling norm of public justice. Government tends to see itself as the representative of popular wills and the broker of competing interests rather than as the *authority* for establishing public justice within a political community that has its own special identity as a public realm in contrast to all private realms.

Another way we can illuminate the meaning of public justice as a norm is to describe more fully the identity of the public realm. A political community will manifest justice when it is characterized by a healthy public interaction of all kinds of non-public groups and persons. In other words, the political community is a definite public legal community that nevertheless cannot be everything; it cannot be a totalitarian collective that destroys or overruns every non-public institution and relationship, or else it becomes an unjust monster. If families and schools, businesses and cooperatives, publishers and professional organizations are not related to one another in a healthy harmony while being free to develop their own identity, then the public realm is not just. To put it another way, the political community is more than a mass of individual citizens ruling themselves through their majority will. It is a community of communities, a public interlacement of hundreds of different groups, institutions, associations, families, and personal relationships.

A just public law, then, is one that advances the public good—not one that promotes education at the expense of families, or encourages business growth at the expense of the environment. Public justice is a norm that functions precisely by guiding government to advance the *whole* public realm, not simply a part of it. The public is not merely consumers who need more products or consumer protection. It is not merely workers who need employment or worshipers who need freedom of religious practice. The public is all citizens considered from the perspective of their membership in the territorial community that is governed by the laws of its public authorities.

The "public realm" has come into full view during the past several centuries through a process whereby it has been distinguished from both private property ownership and ecclesiastical institutions. At one point in history a ruler had public authority by virtue of his private property ownership; feudal lords were "public" masters over everyone in their "private" domains. For centuries public realms were also defined in large part by the "true religion" that an emperor, or church, or lord imposed on a territory.

Today in the United States we are aware that citizenship is not determined or circumscribed by any particular church establishment or by coincidence with any official's private property. Churches, private properties, families, and voluntary and other private associations are all participants in the public realm, but they do not identify the public realm. *Public justice requires, then, that public laws should govern persons, non-public institutions, and relationships among persons and institutions in a way that gives each one its due.* The public authorities should favor no private person or interest, nor should they attempt to overrun or take over the life and authority of non-public institutions and relationships. The political community is a public community that ought to be limited to its public identity and responsibility. It has no right to become whatever it wants to become, even if a majority of the people want it to grow in all directions. On the other hand, a public political community has every right to take shape, through its government, as a strong and definite community of public justice which is not captured or controlled by any private interest.

Government in the political community should be limited not simply by formal restraints and procedures but by the actual public identity of the political community itself. Government authority is a public—not a private—authority. Government touches everyone within the territory of the political community because all citizens are subject to public law and authority. But government should touch everyone only in a public capacity—not by totalitarian control. Public government should be universal—not totalitarian. The norm of public justice requires authoritative, yet limited, government within the political community.

Pluralism and pluralism

Viewing the political community in this fashion implies its pluralistic character. "Pluralism," however, is another ambiguous word. For example, we pride ourselves on America's pluralistic character, by which we mean that we tolerate all kinds of religious confessions, allow freedom of speech, and permit more than one political party to exist. While it is true that the United States is pluralistic in these respects, it is certainly the case that the public realm is not as pluralistic as the non-public areas of American life. We do indeed tolerate many different churches, publications, and expressions of cultural diversity. But our political community at local, state, and federal levels does not display the same degree of pluralism. In fact, there is one sense in which the American Republic is designed to promote public unity at the expense of public diversity.

America's founding fathers believed that a state or nation could only function well if it could act with a single moral will. Thomas Jefferson argued that just as a human body is moved by a single will, so the body politic requires a single will, and that will is to be found in the decisions of the *majority* of its voting citizens. In other words, instead of defining the *unity* of the body politic in terms of its public legal character, Jefferson and others thought in terms of the Republic's moral will, using the analogy of a person. Instead of allowing the norm of public justice to determine the framework for civic expression, they wanted the majority will to determine what would be publicly just.

For this reason American political leaders have been more concerned about the means for arriving at majority representation and majority decisions than about the full public representation of all the diverse groups and viewpoints present within American life. Jefferson even hoped that a public school system would help to produce uniform republican citizens with a common rational view of life, thereby helping to eliminate the diverse and peculiar religious notions which children inherit from parents and priests. Those diverse, pluralistic "notions" threatened to be divisive in the Republic, in Jefferson's view. The school would help to homogenize American citizens so that civic unity could come to expression from out of a common rational will.

In other words, on the one hand the impulse of American political life has been to encourage diversity and pluralism *in private life.* Yet on the other hand, an equally strong impulse has existed to homogenize and unify *public life* by means of majoritarian and uniform policies and procedures. As a consequence, for example, minority groups have a difficult time achieving meaningful political representation because only majorities can win elections in our system of representation. The government discriminates against non-public schools which represent a pluralizing factor rather than a homogenizing factor in public life. Laws are passed by Congress and state legislatures to establish the will of the majority rather than to organize a healthy public framework within which pluralistic diversity can unfold.

The point is that the United States is not as pluralistic as we might like to think. If a political community is going to manifest justice, it cannot create an artificial public unity that fails to reflect a harmonization of the real plurality of groups and viewpoints that exist within its borders. Merely to allow individuals the right to compete for control of the one majority will does not guarantee freedom of public participation to all citizens.

True pluralism is needed in public—not just in private—life. In this respect the principle of *proportional justice* needs to be acknowledged as part of the norm of *public* justice. Different groups, viewpoints, and segments of the population need public representation *in proportion to their numbers* if they are going to be truly free to contribute to the public trust. Without all groups and viewpoints being assured of effective political representation, a political community cannot be just but will only reflect the best or the worst that a compromising majority can come up with. There are other dimensions of public justice as well—distributive justice, retributive justice, and so on. Our purpose here is simply to illustrate how important it is to orient our political thinking toward the norm of justice.

Another primary dimension of pluralism might be called the pluralism of social structures, institutions, associations, and organizations. This goes back to our discussion in the previous section. A political community is different from a school, a family, a church, a business enterprise, or a professional association. Public justice can exist only if the laws and policies of government do justice to the reality of those diverse, non-public social realities.

The fact that in some respects the American Republic has stressed unity over diversity means that the political representatives of "the people" have frequently tended to develop public policies as if "the people" were a homogeneous mass of *individuals.* Far too little thought has been given by governments at all levels to the nature of families, schools, churches, hospitals, voluntary associations, business corporations, labor unions, and dozens of other non-public social entities. Public policies often reflect the homogenized, undifferentiated, majoritarian outlook of policy makers rather than the structural diversity which actually exists in American social life.

Public justice demands that true pluralism be nurtured in public as well as in private life—not just freedom for individuals to compete for control of the public's majority will, but room for diverse groups of citizens to participate in political life in proportion to their numbers. Public justice also demands that the government deal properly and justly with the real diversity of non-public institutions and associations that exist. Justice in the political community requires both kinds of pluralism.

Questions and Suggestions for Discussion

1. Do you consider citizenship to be membership in a political community? Do you consider it to be subjection to authority? What else?
2. Take time in the group to discuss terms such as "state,"

"nation," "government," "society," and "political community." What have those terms suggested to you in the past? Do the words "political community" help to define and suggest a more normative understanding of political life?

3. What difficulties do you see in relating biblical teaching to contemporary politics, given the fact that political life has changed so much in the past 2000 years?

Additional Suggestions for Group Discussion

4. Do citizens ever have the right to revolt against political authorities?
5. Can civil disobedience ever be justified?
6. On the basis of what you have read here, and drawing on your experience, take a specific public policy issue and try to arrive at a conclusion about what should be done in response to the norm of public justice rather than in response to interest-group competition or to the national interest.
7. Are you at all sympathetic to the idea of public funding for a wide variety of school systems? What problems and benefits do you see in it?
8. If pluralistic diversity is encouraged in public life, how can unity be preserved? What kind of unity should exist in the political community? Is the United States sufficiently pluralistic?

For Further Reading

Not much has been written from a Christian point of view on the nature of the public political community, subject to the norm of public justice. Bernard Zylstra's article "The Bible, Justice and the State," listed at the end of Chapter 2, is a good starting point. Bob Goudzwaard's book *A Christian Political Option,* listed at the end of Chapter 4, has some helpful insights. James Skillen's articles, also listed at the end of Chapter 4, shed some light on international politics from a Christian point of view. A more scholarly book along these lines is Herman Dooyeweerd's *The Christian Idea of the State* (Nutley, N.J.: The Craig Press, 1968). Dooyeweerd's book should be read in conjunction with an introduction to his philosophy, the best of which is L. Kalsbeek, *Contours of a Christian Philosophy: An Introduction to Herman Dooyeweerd's Thought* (Toronto: Wedge Publishing Foundation, 1975). Indirectly, a great deal of help can be derived from reading Bob Goudzwaard's two books listed at the end of Chapter 1, *Aid for the Overdeveloped West* and *Capitalism and Progress,* and also H. Evan Runner's *Scriptural Religion and Political Task,* listed at the end of Chapter 2.

For those who want to read scholarly works on the history of Western political thought and the influence of Christianity on the thinking and practice of politics, the following books are suggested:

John H. Hallowell, *Main Currents in Modern Political Thought* (New York: Holt, Rinehart and Winston, 1950).

Robert A. Nisbet, *Quest for Community* (New York: Oxford University Press, 1953).

Walter Ullmann, *Medieval Political Thought* (Baltimore: Penguin Books, 1975).

Also of value as general scholarly works dealing with the nature of the state and the relationship of Christianity to the state are the books by Thomas G. Sanders *(Protestant Concepts of Church and State)* and Donald J. Wolf *(Toward Consensus)*, mentioned at the end of Chapter 2.

For study of the American political tradition, not particularly from a Christian point of view, the following books will prove helpful:

Peter L. Berger and Richard John Neuhaus, *To Empower People: The Role of Mediating Structures in Public Policy* (Washington, D.C.: American Enterprise Institute, 1977).

Berger and Neuhaus look at public policy from the standpoint of its effect on communities and institutions such as the family, the church, the neighborhood, and voluntary associations. They call these the "mediating structures" and recommend that public policy ought to strengthen rather than weaken the mediating structures.

Richard Hofstadter, *The American Political Tradition* (New York: Random House Vintage Books, 1948).

This is a classic portrait of some great leaders and great periods in American history, from the pre-revolutionary era to President Franklin D. Roosevelt.

Walter Lippmann, *The Public Philosophy* (New York: Mentor Books, 1955).

Lippmann was a great journalist and student of political life in America. In this book he analyzes the gradual loss of a "public philosophy" in the Western democracies, and particularly in the United States.

Alexis de Tocqueville, *Democracy in America,* edited and abridged with an Introduction by Andrew Hacker (New York: Washington Square Press, 1964).

De Tocqueville came from France in the nineteenth century to visit the United States. His published reflections after the visit became a classic that is still being discussed and studied. If one does not have time to read the full text, one should at least read an abridged version.

Garry Wills, *Inventing America: Jefferson's Declaration of Independence* (New York: Random House Vintage Books, 1978).

A recently published scholarly book that has won several book awards. The critics judge it to be the best reinterpretation of Jefferson in decades. It helps to explain the foundations of American politics in a new way.

4

Working Together

Taking public life seriously

In the first chapter we concluded that a great need in our day is for Christians to begin making a distinctive contribution to political life because the dominant ideologies, programs, and policies manifest so many signs of crisis and because present Christian attitudes and appoaches are part of the problem. In the second chapter we saw that the biblical revelation calls us to respond to the Lord in service with our whole lives, including our political lives. Chapter 3 brought us to a direct consideration of political community and the norm of public justice.

We could say at this point in our study that two main forces are driving us to a single important conclusion. Both the crises of our day, including the impotence and confusion of Christians, as well as the biblical call to integral and consistent service to God and neighbor, require that we *work together* as Christians to help give shape to public justice in our country and the world.

The proper motivation for working together can, of course, only come from the power of God's Spirit through His Word as we grow in understanding how every dimension of our lives should be offered up to Christ, the King. The crises of our day cannot, in themselves, show us what to do or give us reasons for acting differently. To the contrary, without the hope of new life in Christ, which opens a normative path to follow, we might as easily come to the conclusion that today's problems are beyond solution, that nothing can be done to solve our predicament. Nevertheless, we have to admit that frequently it is a severe crisis in our immediate situation that forces us to re-evaluate our guiding assumptions, our false hopes, our inconsistent lifestyles, and our superficial Christianity. Thus, we can give thanks to God for calling us to attention through critical events, for shaking us loose from unholy alliances and habits, in order to make us desirous of hearing His Word and serving Him totally in all of life.

Part of our awakening and repentance in the present circumstances should be to realize that we ought to take public life seriously as part of our service to the world. Whatever the reasons for our apathy and lack of concern, we Christians have, for the most part, tended to take our families, our churches, our jobs, and our friendships far more seriously than public life. And in public life we display our most secularistic tendencies as Christians. We accept almost without question the same form of participation in public life as everyone else—reading the same daily and weekly news publications and joining the same political parties and interest groups.

But what happens when public discouragement, distrust, and dissatisfaction arise? What happens when the political parties begin to decline, or when public officials become corrupt, or when the government leads us into illegitimate foreign entanglements? When those developments occur, we usually react in the same way as everyone else. We become apathetic, or react conservatively or rebelliously, or feel trapped as citizens who have no adequate recourse in face of a national or local crisis.

All of this simply demonstrates that *as Christians*, as a body of believers who are supposed to demonstrate unity and love and service in Christ, we have not taken public life seriously on biblical terms. We rise and fall with each election, with each national crisis, with each event that the media tell us is important—in the same way as every other group of citizens. We do not have major organizations or associations through which we can develop distinctive civic responses that have "staying power" for decades and generations. We do not have the organizational means for coming to independent evaluations of public policies from a Christian standpoint. For Christian political efforts we do not contribute even one percent of what we spend on daily newspapers, contributions to the major parties, or postage for our letters to congressional representatives. At first glance, in fact, most of us would probably respond more suspiciously to a Christian political association than we would to Common Cause or to Ralph Nader's consumer interest groups.

But if we are going to heed the biblical word, then this must change. We must admit that apart from Christ we can do nothing (John 15:5), that as Christians we must not refrain from gathering together to stir one another up to good works, yes, even to good political works (Heb. 10:23-25). We must begin working together taking public life seriously because justice requires it, our neighbors depend on it, and the life of the body of Christ cannot come to full maturity without it.

We cannot expect to be able to nurture healthy families, or work in wholesome jobs, or enjoy sound friendships, or worship together in peace with other Christians if we ignore or take lightly the public political community of which we are a part. We must come to acknowledge that in Christ God is offering unique strength, wisdom, peace, and justice to the nations, and that we should be fully engaged as salt and light of the world in public life.

The failure of interest-group politics

It must be admitted from the start, however, that there is a very important characteristic of our American political tradition that works against the kind of political participation which the above argument demands. This characteristic is sometimes referred to as "interest-group politics" or "interest-group liberalism." The word "liberalism" in this sense refers to our American political tradition as a whole, and not to the opposite of "conservatism."

As we noted in the last chapter, the American political system functions in a way that discourages the formation of general, principled, citizens' movements or political parties that are each based on a distinct political philosophy. Instead, it encourages the growth of special interest groups that are organized not because of a shared view of public life and the public welfare but because the participants want to protect and advance a particular private or special interest. Part of the reason for this is the structure of our system of political representation. The official legislative representatives of the people who make laws in Washington and the state capitals are elected from geographical districts that have been defined on a small scale quite arbitrarily. In most cases only one representative is elected, even if he or she does not receive support from 49 percent of the voters. In other words, a representative represents a *district* of people, not necessarily the views or desires of *all the people* in that district.

This system requires additional kinds of political participation and representation on the part of citizens because their views may not coincide with those of their district representative and because their interests are never confined to the electoral district in which they live. Farmers, for example, who are spread across many districts, share a common concern. Industrial workers in many states share an important function in common. All kinds of groups—ethnic, occupational, and more—are spread out across the country. Thus, when Congress or a state legislature begins to construct a bill affecting farming or labor or something else, the farmers or laborers must organize to express their view of the matter. The outcome of this type of activity is the creation of lobbying groups that function as informal, non-elected representatives of particular, special interests. The lobbyists for these groups try to influence all elected representatives, hoping to get them to understand and support their special interest.

This system does not encourage the formation of citizens' groups that are concerned in a comprehensive fashion with the normative task of government and with the interrelationship and harmonization of all issues and interests. Such groups would, in most cases, be composed of citizens spread across the country who hold a common viewpoint on public life and government. Their concern for the broad character of political life and the basic direction of government policy would need to be expressed through general representatives, not a special interest lobby. But the only general representatives we have who do hold the power to act on all issues are those whom we elect from our small geographical electoral districts. Is it too much to expect citizens to develop general, all-purpose lobby groups that can function somewhat as shadow legislatures beside the officially elected representatives?

The history of American politics shows us what happens as a consequence of our system's structure and process. On the one hand the significance of the elected representative gradually declines in relation to the geographical district which he or she represents. Fewer and fewer citizens vote in elections; very few citizens know or care about who their representatives are; and only a few citizens are aware of what their representatives do in Congress or the state legislature. On the other hand the influence of interest groups grows and grows as people scramble to protect or advance a variety of their particular interests in the face of similar actions on the part of other interest groups. Our official representatives now find themselves increasingly preoccupied as individual brokers among a wide variety of unconnected and often competing special interests that fly at them from all over the country, and not just from their own districts. At the same time they are less and less influenced by or even attached to a constituency or party that shares with them a common view of (or approach to) political life in general. The political parties which have in the past functioned to some extent as integrating and coordinating organizations are also declining in influence because they are tied up with the electoral process, not with the interest-group lobbying process.

Precisely the opposite tendency is implied in the argument of the first part of this chapter. The great need of the hour, we have said, is for Christians (but also other groups) to work together as citizens with a common concern for political life as a whole, to encourage one another in an organized way to work for justice throughout the public domain. We need to develop an approach that will deal with all issues and interests in such a way that justice can be done to all of them rather than having one special interest satisfied at the expense of another. But Christians (and most other groups of citizens who might share a common philosophy of public life) are not concentrated in one or more electoral districts. Spread across the country and constituting a minority in most electoral districts, it is difficult for them to elect representatives who will carry with them their shared philosophy of government. Without Christians self-consciously working together, it is almost impossible to do so.

Moreover, we share specific interests with others, even if from a different perspective. Christians are also farmers, laborers, educators, artists, and so forth. Thus, we tend to move with the crowd along the road being built by interest-group liberalism—the public road with a thousand conflicting ruts leading in no common direction, the road that runs on and on without sufficient definition of government's limits or responsibilities, without adequate principled debate among the travelers as to where we are all going, and without any adequate means of nurturing well-informed and dedicated communities of citizens.

Interest-group liberalism fails to define and strengthen a public community of justice. It fails to nurture enduring communities of citizens organized around principled conceptions of government and the public good. If we are going to *work together* as Christians, we will have to face this obstacle squarely and commit ourselves to swim against the mainstream of American political life.

Politics is not for everyone

Working together in politics means not only that we must swim against the stream of interest-group politics by taking the whole of public life seriously on biblical terms but also that we must recognize the diversity of gifts and callings among Christians. Politics as a full-time occupation is not for everyone. Politics may not even be of great interest to many Christians. We could say the same thing about every other area of life. Business, education, science, music, and marriage are not for everyone. What should manifest itself among Christians, however, is a common support for all callings in life so that the entire body of Christ can be strengthened and so that all our neighbors will be blessed.

In order for the body of Christ to grow in health, it is not necessary that every member be a full-time pastor. It is not necessary for everyone to farm in order for all to eat. Education does not require that all become teachers. Nevertheless, if church members do not recognize the need for pastors and refuse to support them, the whole church will suffer. If there are not a few who farm, then none will eat. If no one trains and pays teachers, all will live in ignorance. The point is simply that the complex, differentiated condition of contemporary social life goes hand in hand with the differentiation of special occupations and offices of service. This is important for political life as well as for other areas of life.

American Christians have lived for too long with the notion that a political office can be filled by any well-meaning, rational person. We have not expected any special wisdom or understanding about political life to come from uniquely qualified Christian politicians or from organized Christian political work. We have not looked to see if God has given special gifts of leadership or insight into justice to the young people in our circles. We watch carefully for musical talent, athletic prowess, scientific skills, business acumen, and many other abilities to show up in our children, and then we work hard and go to great expense to help them develop those talents. Unfortunately, we do not work equally hard to develop in them an understanding of and concern for public justice. We apparently do not recognize a need for political service and Christian leadership from those who are called by God into public vocations, and consequently we have not paid the price to help such young people develop their God-given talents.

Not all of us need to enter political vocations. But the ability of God's people to work together in real public service will remain weak and compromised if we do not make sure that *some* Christians can help the rest of us fulfill our civic responsibilities by means of their distinctively Christian political leadership. Working together means *enabling* political wisdom and talents to mature in those whom God has called to such vocations.

Domestic confinement is unacceptable

Most of us possess a significant degree of awareness that the body of Christ is a worldwide, global fellowship. Missionaries in other countries, ecclesiastical gatherings, and other events and contacts make us aware that God's people exist throughout the world. When it comes to political life, however, most of us are almost completely nationalistic. Our chief political goal, some argue, should be to seek America's national interest above all else.

But there are two good reasons why we should not confine ourselves to domestic contacts, priorities and concerns in the political arena. First of all, Christians in other parts of the world have political experience, insights, and wisdom from which we can benefit, and we in turn should be making a contribution, with them and for them, to public justice in every country in the world. Second, the world in which we live is fast becoming a "global village" where fewer and fewer domesic issues are unaffected by or isolated from the international political context.

With regard to the first point, the American political experience has been rich and varied. Even today people throughout the world look to the United States as one of the more admirable forms of democracy. Citizens here learn in school that the American Constitution is and should be a highly venerated human creation. All of this tends to make us self-confident, unware of the diverse character of states in the world, and unwilling to subject our own political life to serious criticism.

Even if we admit that racism has been a serious blight throughout our history, or that the Watergate affair aggravated an already declining confidence in public officials, or that U.S. foreign policy has not always been admirable, still we are likely to conclude that since we are better off here than we would be in the Soviet Union and since we have always found a way to solve our problems in the past and since every country has difficult periods of crisis, we should not overreact to our present agonies.

But this attitude or outlook is one of parochial and nationalistic confinement that Christians must transcend. Of course we are Americans and we should not try to escape or deny that fact. But we are *Christians*, and our Christian connection unites us beyond political borders. We are more than Americans. God's call to serve Him by doing justice did not come first or only to Americans. The body of Christ is politically diversified, not non-political. Christians should be working together to render justice in the various domestic orders of which we are a part, but we should also be working together internationally to strengthen our mutual understanding of justice and our common commitment to serve God and neighbors in public life.

The second reason for not confining ourselves to a purely domestic focus is that such a focus will only keep us from grasping political reality today. Economically, militarily, politically, scientifically, and in countless other ways, domestic affairs in the United States (and elsewhere) are tied up intimately with other countries. If non-Christian habits and perspectives tend to get the best of us in American political life, how much more serious might the problem be at the international level? It would be foolish for us to imagine that a small group of American

Christians could, by itself, sort out and address all the political issues in the world with Christian wisdom and justice. If we intend to deal properly with domestic and international politics, then we must reach out at the beginning for cooperative relationships with Christians in other countries.

We need to look at the world through the eyes of poor Christians in small countries, through the eyes of persecuted Christians in dictatorial states, through the eyes of Christians who have been working together at politics in their own countries for decades and centuries. Moreover, we need to view the United States and our Christian political response here through the eyes of these people. They will frequently be able to help us transcend our parochial attachments and nationalistic blindness.

Christ gave a promise to the meek that they would inherit the earth (Matt. 5:5). The body of Christ is supposed to be a community of love and good works that brings blessing to the world. Our calling and ministry as Christians in-public life is global in character. Our work together should help us become better citizens of our various states while at the same time helping us to become more and more of a global community that transcends domestic confinements.

Questions and Suggestions for Discussion

1. Take time in the group to have each person explain the degree of political participation that he or she has experienced in the past two or three years. Why so much or little? Is there any dissatisfaction with the U.S. system of representation? Is there some awareness of how interest-group politics functions?
2. Do you feel that you do take public life seriously enough? Are there any factors that keep you from doing so? Would you be likely to take it more seriously if you could do so with a trusted group of friends or in an association whose aims and purposes you trust?

3. If Christians were participating in public life in an organized fashion on the basis of Christian principles with which you could agree, would you consider a full-time public vocation (in government service, political organization work, public policy research, political journalism, etc.)?

Additional Suggestions for Group Discussion

4. If you are one who would *not* want to work full-time in politics, what kind of information and contacts would you need to have in order to be a regular supporter of a Christian political association? Do you support any interest groups or civic associations now? Would it make any difference to you if you knew that some Christian political organizations existed?
5. Have you had any contact with Christians in other parts of the world? What kind? In what sense do you think Christians could or should have closer contact and unity across national borders that would be closer than their contact and unity with citizens of their own countries?
6. If there is someone in the group interested in pursuing the question of Christian activity in other parts of the world, consider doing a report for the whole group on Christian political parties in other countries, or on the influence of Christianity in contemporary Latin America, where "liberation theology" is having such a strong impact.

For Further Reading

Helge Brattgard, *God's Stewards: A Theological Study of the Principles and Practices of Stewardship*, translated by Gene J. Lund (Minneapolis: Augsburg Publishing House, 1963).

One of the best studies of the biblical and historical meaning of Christian stewardship. Part II of Chapter Two deals particularly with the people of God as a community of stewards responsible together for what God has entrusted to them.

Christian Political Options (The Hague: Anti-Revolutionary Party, 1979).

A fine collection of essays from Christian politicians and political scholars from various parts of the world. These English-language essays were first presented as speeches at a seminar celebrating the hundredth anniversary of the Anti-Revolutionary Party in the Netherlands. They help to show how Christians have worked together in politics—and should continue to do so.

Enrique Dussel, *History and the Theology of Liberation*, translated by John Drury (Maryknoll, N.Y.: Orbis Books, 1976).

From among Christians in Latin America there is arising a new framework of thought and new modes of action in the political arena. This is one fine example of a Latin American perspective on national and global politics which North Americans should study.

Bob Goudzwaard, *A Christian Political Option*, translated by Herman Praamsma (Toronto: Wedge Publishing Foundation, 1972).

An excellent book introducing some of the primary elements of communal Christian political responsibility, by a Dutch parliamentarian and economist who has been part of a Christian political party that is more than 100 years old.

Michael Harrington, *The Other America: Poverty in the United States* (Baltimore: Penguin Books, 1971).

One of the groups or classes of people that is spread out across America and is quite underrepresented in Congress and the state legislatures is the poorest class. Harrington's classic study helps to explain why poor people do not participate very much in politics.

Hendrik Hart, *The Challenge of Our Age* (Toronto: Wedge Publishing Foundation, 1968).

A broad-ranging examination of some of the main secularizing characteristics of our age, including American pragmatism, scientism, materialism, and individualism. The author urges Christians to work together *in community* in all areas of life.

Theodore Lowi, *The End of Liberalism.*
See the comment on this book at the end of Chapter 1.

Michael Novak, *The Rise of the Unmeltable Ethnics* (New York: Macmillan, 1972).
A lively and insightful discussion of the true diversity of groups that exists in the United States—groups that have not "melted down" into one homogenized mass of Americans. Ethnic identity is one of the characteristics of groups of people that do not live in the same electoral districts.

James H. Olthuis, et al., *Will All the King's Men . . .* (Toronto: Wedge Publishing Foundation, 1972).
Seven essays on the present predicament and responsibility of the church in North America. The essays by Hendrik Hart and Bernard Zylstra are especially helpful in showing the connections between the church as a differentiated organization and the people of God as active agents in all of life.

Paul Schrotenboer, *Man in God's World* (Toronto: Wedge Publishing Foundation, 1968).
An excellent, brief introduction to the meaning of human beings as God's communal stewards of the world. The author explains the meaning of human "offices" and the nature of shared and differentiated responsibility among Christians. This would be an excellent booklet for further study and discussion in a group context.

Ruth K. Scott and Ronald J. Hrebenar, *Parties in Crisis: Party Politics in America* (New York: John Wiley and Sons, 1979).
An up-to-date study (for political science students) of

the contemporary crisis of the traditional political parties. Historical information, statistics, and various arguments are brought together to show the declining influence and significance of political parties in the U.S.

James W. Skillen, "International Justice: Is it Possible?" *International Reformed Bulletin*, 18th year, 1975, No. 62/63, pp. 2-16.

An article designed to look at the "shrinking globe" from the point of view of the mutual responsibility of states for global justice. An attempt is made to show the relevance of biblical, normative thinking for contemporary international politics.

Skillen, "International Interdependence and the Demand for Global Justice," *International Reformed Bulletin*, 20th year, 1977, No. 68, pp. 20-35.

An article for political science students explaining some of the problems in contemporary thinking about the interdependence of nations in the world. The author attempts to show what a Christian approach to the issues would demand at the global level.

5

Building a Movement: The Association for Public Justice

An association of citizens

The Scriptures call us to the service of God through Christ with our whole lives. It is crucial, then, that we work together as Christians in every area of life so that we can practice biblical discipleship. In order to work together, however, we must know what to do and how to do it, and therefore we must ask: Does Christian cooperation require formal organizations, and more specifically, does it require Christian political organizations?

To answer this question, let us return for a moment to the important issue raised in the second chapter regarding the differentiation of social life into relatively independent institutions and relationships such as families, schools, businesses, and political communities. In our contemporary historical situation, we live in a highly differentiated society. In fact, one of our biggest problems as Christians is that we do not experience enough of the unity of life under Christ's Lordship because our lives are divided into so many units that are not adequately connected. But if God intended to have His human stewards discover and develop the full diversity of the creation, then a highly differentiated society is not necessarily illegitimate or anti-normative. On the contrary, what is wrong with our present social order is not its differentiated character but the extent to which human beings have been shaping each area of life in ways that violate the norms of God for His creatures.

To be specific, it is good that an emperor no longer decides what the "correct" religion should be for everyone in his empire; it is good that scientists and artists are free to pursue their work without having church authorities dictate (on non-scientific and non-artistic grounds) what is true and beautiful; and we should welcome the fact that families are free to arrange their own internal lives rather than having them controlled by a feudal master or a slave owner. In other words, as Christians we can welcome the differentiation of social life.

But at the same time we should be critical of our modern political communities or states in which authorities and citizens do not recognize that political life should be shaped in accordance with God's norms for public life. We should be unhappy about the free scientific and artistic work that does not seek truth and beauty. We should weep at the failure of many husbands, wives, and parents to love one another and their children. In other words, we should reject differentiation that does not subject itself to the will of God.

If we are going to face our present situation as responsible Christians, then we do not want to ignore or oppose the differentiation process; rather, we should work for the proper, biblical realization and renewal of life in every differentiated sphere as well as for the realization of a healthy integration of all areas of life. We should not seek an end to scientific freedom, or family independence, or ecclesiastical separation from the state. Instead we should work for free science that is truthful, independent families that are loving, and churches separated from state control that are biblically obedient.

With regard to public life, which is our particular concern here, this implies something very important. Just as Christians must look for ways to work together according to biblical norms in churches, families, businesses, and countless other relationships, so too we must ask how we can best work together as citizens for public justice. The implication of this argument is that we *ought to accept* the differentiated political community as a legitimate reality. Citizenship in a political community is not only a fact that we can accept, it is also an office that can be properly distinguished from our family memberships, occupational involvements, and ecclesiastical identities. Therefore the fulfillment of our civic responsiblities calls for the kind of action that is appropriate to citizenship, and not the kind that would belong to ecclesiastical life, or scientific work, or the family.

This is why it is important, even necessary, for us to organize associations of citizens specifically for Christian political action rather than trying to fulfill our civic reponsibilities through the churches, or through private philanthropic organizations, or through general social action agencies. Given the specific identity of the modern political community, we need an association for public justice that is defined in terms of Christian citizenship rather than in terms of church membership, ethnic tradition, or occupational identity. Associations based on occupational, ecclesiastical, or ethnic identity or those oriented toward general Christian social action, will either have a special-interest character in the public realm or will be too diffuse in their focus to be able to direct all their energies toward the specific task of public justice that belongs to governments and citizens in the political community.

Of course, many other aspects of Christian service will not be accomplished by a Christian political organization. But that is how it should be. Churches should carry on their ecclesiastical work; families should take care of their responsibilities; hospitals and relief agencies need to work for the alleviation of pain, hunger, and suffering; publishing organizations need to produce everything from newspapers to scholarly books; and other organizations and institutions should fulfill their callings. A Christian political association cannot and should not try to do everything for Christians. Political action is not the first, or highest, or only responsibility belonging to Christians. A political association should accept its limited task with humility as one dimension of Christian service in God's multi-dimensional world.

Three prongs on one fork

If we accept the fact that Christian political responsibility calls for associations qualified by citizenship, then it is appropriate to ask about the nature of such an association. At this point bear in mind that an association has to grow, and we can anticipate its mature character only by looking ahead from the vantage point of its beginning. Thus, while it is legitimate to ask what a mature Christian political association should be, we must not expect that an immature one will be able to accomplish all the tasks of a mature one.

Moreover, a fully mature, explicitly Christian, politically comprehensive organization has never existed in the United States, so we do not have an example to look back upon in this country. In the absence of a more mature Christian political organization, a look at the Association for Public Justice can help us to reflect on the important issues at stake in building a political movement.

Founded in 1970, the Association for Public Justice (APJ) is attempting to develop a three-pronged approach. Consider a fork with three prongs as a metaphor to represent the Association. First, consider the fork as a whole. Citizenship encompasses everyone within a territorial political community (with the typical exceptions of visitors, aliens, etc.). All citizens in the United States are bound together as members of the same public legal community. For this reason a mature political association ought to be oriented toward the full range of political life in the United States and draw its members from the entire country. There may be times when localized organizations, confined to a city or state, are appropriate, but local and state associations should be related to a national organization in a way that reflects the relationship of states and cities to the United States. Christians who are citizens of the United States should work together in a Christian political association that is coextensive with the political community in which they are citizens. That kind of association would be the fork—a single entity aiding and representing Christian citizens in the fulfillment of their political responsibility. It is the intention of the Association for Public Justice to be that kind of association.

The first prong on the fork can be thought of as the job of educating and organizing citizens. In order for Christians to work together, they must grow together into a common political mind and be able to function together in one organization. APJ is trying to build a real community of understanding and purpose among its members on the basis of explicitly formulated principles and guidelines. Books, newsletters, pamphlets, conferences, meetings, and more are involved in the promotion of its educational and organizational life. Moreover, some kind of organizational structure is essential, even if it remains quite flexible and diversified. A national board of directors related to local groups and regional coordinators is the basic structure that APJ is using. Some other structure might also work. But whatever the structure, a Christian community of citizens must keep on growing together on the basis of a Christian understanding of and approach to political life.

At the early stages of its development APJ members have found that not all of their civic responsibilities can be aided or addressed by the Association. Maturation of a political organization takes time. Fresh policies and approaches cannot be created overnight. Members have to give much and receive little at the early stages of development. But the first prong that must exist is a community of members organized throughout the country, dedicated to the common task of Christian political service.

The second prong, dependent upon and supportive of the first, is a research and policy-formulating group. A common political cause among Christians is not possible without the development of specific programs and policies that emerge from the unique perspective on political life that Christians share. But research into contemporary politics which can bring forth new programs and policy proposals requires the full-time work of people who are specially qualified for it. As we pointed out in Chapter 4, politics is not for everyone, but it is essential for some people to work full-time in this area. A group of research associates is an essential component of the Association for Public Justice, and in its maturity this prong of the fork will take the form of a policy research center that can deal with every aspect of political life and public policy from a Christian point of view.

Notice the close connection between the discussion in Chapter 3 and this second prong of a Christian political association. Public justice is a norm or guiding principle to which we should respond in our political service. Unfortunately, most policy formulation in the U.S. comes from centers that are tied in with specific, limited interests or with research programs that are not oriented toward the norm of public justice. The research center of a Christian political association should be able to offer something quite unique—program and policy proposals formulated as responses to the norm of public justice and connected with one another to show the integral character of justice for the entire public realm. The work of such a center should not only reflect the life of the Association but also strengthen the understanding and commitment of its members.

The third prong of APJ is its work to influence government directly. This can take the form of presenting testimonies before Congressional committees, working on cases in the courts, trying to explain a particular policy option to an official in one of the bureaucracies, or any number of other actions.

At times this work might be carried on by a full-time employee of the Association; at other times it might be accomplished through the coordinated efforts of the members. Appropriate strategies and programs for influencing the government have to be developed that fit the

Association's particular stage of development and capabilities. Whatever the specific programs, a Christian political association should want to direct its energies, in as many ways as possible. toward the authorities who are responsible for making, enforcing, and adjudicating laws for the sake of public justice.

Together, these three prongs, closely coordinated, constitute the Association for Public Justice. Its aim is to grow into an integral, comprehensive, political organization that can perform the differentiated function of Christian political service. It should be able to serve Christians, including full-time political servants as well as those who are occupied primarily with other responsibilities. It should be able to aid public authorities both by offering sound proposals and by opposing unjust laws and actions. It should seek to serve all citizens by working for just laws for everyone and by bearing testimony to the righteousness and peace of Christ's Kingdom.

Local, regional, and national presence

A Christian political movement in the United States that is coextensive with U.S. citizenship requires a national organization. Yet clearly a national organization cannot exist without leadership and organization at many levels. Furthermore, many political issues are primarily local or state issues that must be handled by local or state groups or chapters of a national organization. Thus, a Christian political organization needs to be unified in terms of its membership, basis, purpose, and general program, as well as diversified and flexible with respect to its structure, leadership, and particular activities at many levels.

The Association for Public Justice has adopted a particular strategy with regard to the development of associational life and leadership at different levels. The Board of Directors of the Association, through its executive staff, is working to develop the membership, the general principles, the broad framework, the general strategy, and the policy research potential of the

Association as a whole. At the same time, realizing that most of the Association's life will occur at levels where its members can get together in face-to-face study groups, action groups, seminars, conferences, and planning sessions, the Board has appointed a group of regional coordinators that can personally introduce others to the Association and help to organize their activities in ways that will be most useful in each situation. From out of this kind of personal and flexible coordination of activities, a variety of types of local chapters, regional coordinators, and other structures can arise that will accurately reflect and nurture the life and strengths of the Association.

Members of APJ are encouraged to do everything possible to fulfill their civic responsibilities both by taking up opportunities for involvement that are sponsored or directed by the Association as well as by engaging in activities that are not part of the Association's program. APJ, like any political organization, has its own maturation tempo. At certain points it will be ahead of some of its members, offering them more than they need or want; at other points it will be behind some of them, offering less than they need or want by way of insight and programs. Maximum growth for both the individuals and the Association will take place as members bring into the Association the wisdom they gain from experiences outside of it, and as they work together to help it come to its own maturity. Not every political responsibility which members have can be fulfilled through APJ, but the Association can benefit from every experience and insight that its members gain.

As the Association matures, integrating more and more people and programs into its three-pronged indentity, it will be in an ever stronger position both to discover and to nurture the leadership that emerges at local, regional, and national levels. That leadership will manifest itself in the form of policy research expertise, speaking and writing talents, organizing and administrative abilities, insight into public justice, and more. The Association's Board will continue to provide general oversight and to formulate broad strategy for the organization's many leaders to implement at all levels in a wide variety of ways.

Whether or not the experience of the Association for Public Justice will prove to be helpful to other organizations, it would seem that a Christian political association should be aware of its own rate of growth and maturation; should be careful not to overestimate or underestimate its capabilities at each stage of development; should encourage its members to contribute to its growth by means of their experiences gained outside as well as inside the association; should strive for a common Christian basis, purpose, program, and membership coextensive with territorial citizenship; and should nurture its membership at local, regional, and national levels in ways that will strengthen personal interrelationships, diverse political talents, and the spontaneous efforts of members at all levels.

Organized for action

The final point that should be made with regard to the development of a Christian political movement is that it must be organized for political action. Although this might seem obvious at first glance, it is important to remember that an organized Christian political association is not a typical phenomenon in American life.

When Christians get together to organize something, it is usually ecclesiastical or educational work that concerns them. Schools, colleges, churches, magazines, book companies, and evangelistic associations are fairly typical expressions of organized Christian efforts. Christian labor unions, Christian professional organizations, and Christian political associations are not so typical. Consequently, when Christians do begin to get together out of concern for political life, they might unconsciously begin to shape their efforts after the pattern of an educational or evangelistic venture.

Of course, genuine Christian political action cannot have the character of mindless activism, focused only on an immediate issue and unconscious of the principles and historical circumstances involved. But "activism" is not the only danger to avoid. Christian citizens must also avoid the danger of *not* being political in their organized efforts. It is possible for Christians to talk about politics in an organized way, to philosophize about politics in an organized way, and even to write about politics in an organized way, and to imagine that their Christian obligation is fulfilled through talk and declarations *about* politics. But there is more to political service than talking and writing.

Another danger, of course, is that Christians will organize a political association which plans to be fully engaged in politics but which is hardly distinguishable from existing political parties or interest groups. It might call its effort Christian while its principles, vision, aims, and common basis for membership differ little from the liberal or conservative efforts that abound in the Western world.

The way to avoid the danger of activism, on the one hand, and of too much talk, on the other hand, is to organize for action in a way that is specifically and definitely political according to thoroughly Christian principles. In this sense, political action must be defined far more broadly than usual. Indeed, reading, talking, writing, and doing research about politics are important aspects of political *action* if they are oriented toward the clarification and formulation of a Christian political perspective and program. Political action is not merely voting, marching, and campaigning for some specific candidate or cause. Nevertheless, reading, talking, writing, and doing research in a political way must be oriented toward the total purpose of promoting public justice in the political community. And this means working to create, enforce, and adjudicate laws that will bring justice to all.

Questions and Suggestions for Discussion

1. Do you believe that organizations are a good and constructive part of our human response to God's commandments, or do you believe that organizations only get in the way of genuine human relationships and service? Why?
2. Spend some time in the group discussing the meaning of the historical differentiation of social institutions and relationships. Do members of the group understand the meaning of "differentiation" in reference to society? Do all agree that a differentiated social order is not necessarily bad or anti-normative? If not, why not?
3. Do you think that the United States is too big or too old for a Christian political movement to emerge and gain influence in it?

Additional Suggestions for Group Discussion

4. Given the present degrees of interest in political life among the members of your discussion group, how would you see yourselves participating in an organization such as the Association for Public Justice? As observers, as individual members, as an organized local group, as contributors to policy research, or as something else?
5. Suggest that someone in the group (or several persons) who is (are) interested in the development of a Christian political association do some investigation into the development of other political organizations in the U.S. and other parts of the world. Discussion of those findings could prove useful in comparison with what has been outlined here.
6. For one or more sessions of your discussion, invite into your midst someone who is responsible for administering a complex organization, perhaps a city government, a political party, a business, a university, or some other large structure. Ask questions about the way in which such an organization works, changes, and deals with all the people working in it. After the inter-

view, pursue discussion among yourselves, trying to discover the important differences between a political organization and a non-political organization.

7. What kind of healthy relationship ought to exist among churches, families, Christian schools, other Christian organizations, and a Christian political association? In other words, how should a proper diversity of Christian institutions and associations be interrelated in a way that demonstrates the unity of the body of Christ under His Lordship?

For Further Reading

W. N. Chambers and Walter D. Burnham, editors, *The American Party Systems* (New York: Oxford University Press, 1967).

A collection of scholarly essays describing and analyzing the primary political organizations in American history—the different political parties—and the way they have functioned at different periods in history.

Christian Political Options (The Hague: Anti-Revolutionary Party, 1979).

See the comments at the end of Chapter 4.

Maurice Duverger, *Political Parties: Their Organization and Activity in the Modern State,* translated by Barbara and Robert North (London: Methuen, 1969).

First published in French by the author in 1954, this has remained a classic study of the structure and function of modern political parties. Given the crisis and decline of American parties in recent years, some of Duverger's analysis does not fit the American situation very well now.

Jacques Ellul, *The Political Illusion*, translated by Konrad Kellen (New York: Random House Vintage Books, 1967).

A critique of modern democratic political systems by

a French Protestant sociologist and political official. His argument is that the belief that citizens can effectively participate in political life today is an illusion.

Michael P. Fogarty, *Christian Democracy in Western Europe: 1820-1953* (London: Routledge and Kegan Paul, 1957).

One of the very best books on the emergence and development of Christian Democratic political parties and other Christian organizations in western Europe.

Alexander Hamilton, James Madison, and John Jay, *The Federalist Papers*, selected and edited by Roy P. Fairfield, second edition (Garden City, N.Y.: Doubleday Anchor Books, 1966).

This selection from the *Federalist Papers*, or the complete edition, should be read by those interested in knowing what the main lines of argument and discussion were during the period of the formation of the U.S. federal Constitution. It will become quite clear in the reading of these essays how little thought was given to the nature of political community, public justice, and the principles necessary for nurturing political organizations among different groups of citizens.

R.E.M. Irving, *The Christian Democratic Parties in Western Europe* (London: George Allen and Unwin, 1979), and Irving, *Christian Democracy in France* (London: George Allen and Unwin, 1973).

Two excellent studies of the development of Christian politics in Europe in the nineteenth and twentieth centuries.

"Justice for All: The Basis and Vision of the Association for Public Justice," a pamphlet published by APJ, Box 5769, Washington, D.C. 20014.

The basic principles of APJ, drawn from its constitution, are printed here, along with a brief section of explanation and commentary on each part. This would be an excellent pamphlet for group discussion in the context of the present chapter, or after the group has finished reading and discussing this whole book.

"Justice for Representation," a pamphlet published by APJ.

After assessing the various aspects of failure in American political participation, the pamphlet goes on to suggest a change in structure that would do proportional justice to all groups of citizens in the United States, encouraging them to participate meaningfully in public life.

Hans Maier, *Revolution and Church: The Early History of Christian Democracy, 1789-1901* (Notre Dame: University of Notre Dame Press, 1965).

Another good study of the development of Christian Democratic movements and parties in Europe, in this case focused on the earliest period.

Frank Vanden Berg, *Abraham Kuyper: A Biography* (St. Catharines, Ontario: Paideia Press, 1978).

Kuyper was the founder and organizer of the first Christian political party in the Netherlands. He was also a churchman, educator, journalist, and leader on other fronts. This biography tells of Kuyper's political efforts and also shows how he understood the relationship between a political organization and other institutions and organizations in a differentiated society.

Edward Vanderkloet, editor, *A Christian Union in Labour's Wasteland* (Toronto: Wedge Publishing Foundation, 1979).

This collection of essays edited by the executive director of the Christian Labour Association of Canada provides helpful insight into the motivation, principles, and structure of a Christian association in the area of business and labor.

Edmund Wilson, *To the Finland Station: A Study in the*

Writing and Acting of History (Garden City, N.Y.: Doubleday Anchor Books, 1940).

This classic biographical history covers much of the past 200 years of political life from the point of view of those who made history. Wilson is particularly concerned with the influence of revolutionary movements led by people such as Saint-Simon, Fourier, Marx, Lenin, and Trotsky.

6

What Are the Consequences?

In the previous chapters we considered some of the primary characteristics of an organized, Christian contribution to political life. Now let us look at five different kinds of consequences that might flow from this approach to political service—consequences for organizational structure, for program aims, for a particular policy issue, for an aspect of the community's structure, and for what cannot be achieved.

Organizational structure

Precisely because of a particular understanding of the Christian life, of the historical differentiation process, of the political community, of the task of gevernment, and of the responsibility of citizens, the Association for Public Justice organized itself as a comprehensive, three-pronged, political organization. It consciously decided not to become a narrow interest group, or a merely local organization, or a general social action agency. Moreover, APJ has developed an internal structure of authority that is a consequence of its whole approach and outlook. A national organization that wants to be unified by a common Christian perspective and by dedication to biblical norms is quite different from a political organization that gets its norms, directions, and purpose from the will of its members.

The Association for Public Justice is organized with a national Board of Directors as the final decision-making authority. The Board members are selected because of their insight into public justice and their ability to help the Association realize its normative purpose of promoting public justice. The Board members are elected by the members of the Association after having been nominated by the Board following recommendation from the Association members. In other words, a triple screening process is followed, involving everyone in the Association, in order to obtain Board members who can make a maximum contribution to the normative guidance of the Association. First of all, each year when the rotating terms of a few of the Board members draw to a close, members of the Association suggest names to the Board for nomination. (No Board member can serve more than two consecutive three-year terms.) The Board then, in the second step, discusses the qualifications of various candidates in the light of the six principled affirmations that constitute the basis of APJ (see Appendix). It nominates those whom it believes are qualified, making sure that more nominees are selected than there are offices to be filled. Finally, in the third step, Association members elect (by written ballot) several Board members from the list of nominees.

The national Board of Directors, thus elected, has the authority to make decisions about hiring the exective staff and to determine the structure and basic direction of the organization at all levels, including the appointment of regional coordinators, the development of local and state organizations, and so forth. In other words, the Board, as a central authority, has the freedom and responsibility to build a unified political association of many distinct parts and levels. The test of a good Board is its ability and wisdom to nurture in an *authoritative* but *nonauthor-*

itarian fashion all the diverse talents that enter the Association toward the end of realizing the purpose of a Christian political organization.

Both the structure of authority as well as the general character of APJ as a three-pronged political organization are consequences that flow directly and self-consciously from a Christian view of human stewardship in God-given offices of responsibility. The ultimate authority for a differentiated Christian political association, the same as for any other human organization, should be the normative Word of God. That authority can best be heeded by developing an organization in which those with insight into the nature of political life and into the authoritative norms of God for politics can fill the offices of leadership in the organization. No structure can give guarantees against abuse and corruption, but APJ believes that its organizational identity and its structure of authority can contribute to the proper fulfillment of Christian political responsibility if its members, Board of Directors, and staff persons will work together in openness to God's dynamic Word.

Program aims

The basic program plans of the Association for Public Justice are a second consequence of its understanding of Christian political service. For example, APJ has decided that all three prongs of its purpose ought to unfold together in a balanced harmony rather than separately in different stages.

Instead of developing a think tank or research center first and then trying later to build a citizens' movement or an arm for influencing government, it was decided that a comprehensive political association is necessary from the start, even it if must grow more slowly and gradually, so that policy research can be directly related to a developing Christian community of political action.

Another option would have been to try to rally together a citizens' movement around an immediate cause or personality, and then to hope that a large enough membership might make it possible to do some careful study and research later on.

Or a third approach would have been to seek funds for one or two persons to try to influence goverment in a particular direction, and then to use any successes as the basis for building a citizens' movement or a research group or both.

All those options and others were rejected after some experimentation and false starts because it became clear that the Association ought not to aim, first of all, for a program of big growth, or big influence, or big ideas, but should instead aim to develop a movement that can do the job required of citizens in the public order. To fulfill that aim and to develop a proper, balanced, comprehensive program for public justice, it would be necessary to avoid short cuts and half measures. A comprehensive program of political education, association building, policy research, and government influence would have to mature in a balanced way so that a single, principled, mature organization of Christian citizens could grow on a firm foundation and be able to serve the public good for a long time to come. Thus, the program has included serious policy research, publications, seminars, conferences, testimonies before Congress, local development, and a number of other activities.

Closely related to this was another program decision *not* to become a political party. There were two primary reasons for this decision. First, the political parties in the United States today are largely electoral machines. They do very little to aid the growth of mature political participation among citizens in the sense that we have been discussing it. Very little defines party membership or holds members together in the parties. In most respects they do not function as associations but only as the tools for electoral purposes. It would be very difficult to communicate the comprehensive and unique purpose of APJ to people if they thought of it as just "another party."

The second reason is the system of representation that

exists in the United States. We referred to this briefly in Chapter 4 and will return to it again in the next section of the present chapter. Our system of electoral representation encourages the formation of the type of party that can win the majority of votes in separate geographical districts. A party that cannot expect to win a majority of votes in a large number of districts is not likely to get very far in anything else that it does, since winning elections is the chief aim of the parties. As an association, attempting to develop a community of Christian citizens across the whole country who share a common, comprehensive perspective and civic commitment, APJ would exist at cross-purposes with a political party structure that is oriented almost solely toward winning majority elections in small, single-member electoral districts.

The program aims of the Association for Public Justice are both more principled and broader than those of interest groups, political parties, think tanks, and lobby organizations. To fulfill its calling, it must develop a unique program.

A policy issue

A third consequence that follows from the kind of approach that APJ has taken to Christian political service can be seen in one specific issue that it has dealt with in some detail, namely, education. This was the first issue that the Association examined in an attempt to arrive at a better framework for public policy. As the Associaton matures and has time to handle more public issues, it should become possible in every case to show how its policy conclusions are a consequence of its Christian principles and purpose.

The issue of education is important for several reasons. First, a government's policies regarding education must always deal with the important institutions of the family, the school, and in some cases the church. Thus the issue is one that concerns the interrelationships of public and non-public institutions as well as the general questions of finance, equity, federal structure, and public benefit.

In the second place, educational questions are enduring questions. The specific issue one year might be the financing of education, another year the quality of education, and another year the creation of a separate federal department of education. But the basic concern is alive year after year. Therefore, thorough study of educational policy at one point will bear fruit year after year as new aspects of the same question receive attention at different times.

Finally, the issue of education is important because it helps to spotlight the problems of pluralism and the task of government in the public order. Not only is there a plurality of institutions related to education, as we noted in the first point above, but there is a plurality of views of education in the United States. This raises several fundamental questions. If the government is concerned about having educated citizens who can serve the public good, does that give it the right to own and run schools that are directed by the will a majority of the citizens? How much freedom should be given to those who want schools that are directed by a different philosophy than that of the dominant public majority? Should parents by allowed not to send their children to school? These and other questions are crying out for new answers in our day.

The Association believes that public justice requires a different basic public structure for education than the one that now exists (see the APJ pamphlet "Justice for Education"). At the present time, local, state, and federal governments assume that governments have the right to establish and run schools and to require the attendance of children at those schools up to a certain age. Taxes are collected in a generally inequitable fashion from property owners to fund these public schools.

Citizens do have a limited right to escape from part of this system. They may set up "private schools" with other monies and send their children to them if the schools meet certain qualifications. But taxpayers do not have a right to escape from paying taxes for the public schools (even if they do not use those schools), nor do they have any educational alternative whatever if they are unable to afford non-public schools.

APJ argues that parents and adult students should have the primary right to arrange schooling for their children and themselves. This would mean the freedom to select the educational agent of their choice without financial or any other penalty. Government, on the other hand, should consider the public welfare from the standpoint of an equitable encouragement of education for all citizens. Schools should be as independent of the government as are the churches—they should be disestablished in the sense that government should not own or operate them as part of its bureaucracy and political process, even at the local level. Different agents of education (different schools) should be free to offer their services without financial penalty.

If the government decides that in order to encourage equitable educational opportunities for all citizens it is necessary to finance schools with public funds, then it should collect those taxes in an equitable fashion and it should distribute its educational tax revenues fairly and equitably to *all* legitimate schools *in proportion* to their service. If parochial schools educate ten percent of the student population, they should receive ten percent of the public funding. If secular community schools are freely selected by fifty percent of the student population, they should receive fifty percent of the tax revenues for education, and so on.

This system would not only recognize and promote the pluralism of worldviews and educational philosophies that exists in America, it would also strengthen the non-public identities of families, schools, and other organizations and institutions. Moreover, this system would strengthen public unity in a legitimate way. Instead of trying to create a general moral unity by a uniform, enforced public education, the government would be strengthening a common commitment to the public legal order in which justice is done to the true diversity that exists. In other words, the real identity of the public, political community as a legal bond of all citizens would be differentiated more clearly from non-public institutions and private communities such as families, schools, churches, and businesses. Common commitment to the public welfare and to public law would be strengthened because the government would be nurturing the real pluralism that exists, and not interfering illegitimately in the non-public rights of families, schools, and so forth.

The structure of the political community

At several points in our study we have raised questions about the structure of the political community, and particularly the legislative branch of government. This has to do with the "internal" identity and character of the political community as compared with its "external" relationships and limits. In the preceding section we suggested that schools ought to be disestablished and placed outside (made external to) direct governmental operation. Now we want to turn our attention to a fourth consequence of a Christian approach to politics by arguing that a change in the *internal* structure of the political community also ought to be made. Once again, we should stress that this is only one example. Other important issues of structural justice could and must be discussed.

The American political system is structured to deal fairly well with several essential characteristics of political life. Its federal structure allows considerable room for handling questions of centralization and decentralization. It also allows for a good balance between the representation of states in the Senate and population density in the House of Representatives. Its division between legislative, executive, and judicial powers allows for a relatively free articulation and exercise of each power without improper interference from the others. The Presidency focuses government in a single highest office which not only expedites executive decisions but also helps to remind us that a political community is a single community of citizens under one public authority (even if that authority is subdivided into many layers of federal, state, and local offices).

What our system does not do very well is to represent different communities of political conviction or different public philosophies in the legislative branches of government. By "communities" of political conviction we do not mean "special interests" but rather communities of thought among citizens about what the task and program of government as a whole ought to be. The main problem is the structure of electoral districts where persons are elected by majority vote (over 50 percent) or plurality vote (more than any other candidate) to the House of Representatives and state legislatures.

This system has two basic faults. First, it draws arbitrary borders for electoral districts around small geographical patches rather than around communities of political perspective and conviction. The assumption seems to be that for public purposes there is only one basic community in America, namely, the entire political community made up of all citizens. Electoral districts, therefore, can be drawn arbitrarily as long as they embrace all citizens. Whereas it is true that there is only one bond of citizenship in a political community, defined by subjection to one government, this is not true with regard to the diverse communities of thought and conviction about *how* that government should function. In other words, what ought to be distinguished is the *single bond* of citizenship under one government from the *many bonds* of conviction about government and citizenship that ought to be represented in government.

The second fault is closely connected with the first: it is the principle of majority rule appled to each arbitrarily defined electoral district. This leads to the election of a representative who might not be the choice of a large portion of the people in his or her district. Those who do not vote for the representative who is elected are, in one sense, disenfranchised. Their votes do not count. In other words, all citizens are not represented as they would like to be represented but only as the majority-rule election principle allows them to be represented. Once again, a distinction ought to be made between unitary government decisions made by majority votes in Congress or legislature, on the one hand, and, on the other hand, the process of voting by citizens to elect representatives—a process that should aim at proper representation of all citizens, not at a majority-rule decision that attempts to create a single majority will of the Republic at the ballot box.

The Association for Public Justice has argued that greater justice could be done to representation if some elements of a system of *proportional representation* would be inaugurated in the United States (see the APJ pamphlet "Justice for Representation"). This change would address both problems just mentioned. As a hypothetical example, if an entire state were defined as a single district instead of being divided into 100 districts for the purpose of electing its state representatives, and if those 100 seats were filled by means of proportional representation on a state-wide basis, then there would be a different result than under the present system. In a strong Democrat state, for example, where the Democrats regularly win 70 or 80 percent of the seats by gaining a majority of votes in 70 or 80 of the small districts (even if they get only 55 or 60 percent of the votes in each of those districts), a different result might occur under the new system. If, state-wide, the Democrats got 60 percent of the vote, they would obtain just 60 out of 100 seats, not 70 or 80. A party that won only 20 percent of the votes, on the other hand, would obtain 20 seats rather than none (or perhaps 1 or 2) as would now be the case. In other words, every vote would count, and all citizens could be represented in a proportion to the number of their votes for the candidates whom they really wanted. A number of parties representing different political views would each have room to function throughout the entire territory being represented and would not be boxed out by an artificial and unrepresentative majority.

If this system were to be adopted at all levels in the country, then simple majoritarianism would be removed from the process of electing representatives. City, state, and federal levels of the political community would begin to see full representation of the diverse communities of political thought and conviction.

The primary point to be made is that a political community of justice cannot be built on the basis of a forced or artificial consensus created by majority-rule elections in districts that do not correspond to the real communities of political thought and conviction in the country. Unified government policies ought to be created by legislators who adequately represent the citizens, following thorough debate and compromise among all contending viewpoints. A system of proportional representation would strengthen the political community by allowing fairer representation of all citizens and by bringing Congress and legislatures face to face with the genuine diversity of political views in the country.

What not to do

Another consequence, to which we can point in conclusion, concerns the strategy that a Christian political association adopts with regard to the use of its own strengths and abilities. In its early development, the Association for Public Justice gave quite a bit of attention to laying its own foundations and to pursuing policy areas such as education and political representation. In the late 1970s APJ was only beginning to develop a strategy for local development and was only beginning to study issues such as energy, the environment, international trade, agriculture, and Indian rights. Countless other issues were left untouched.

The reasons for these limits and accomplishments were several. First, in the 1970s the Association was blessed with certain talents, and not with others. Second, during the same period a solid consensus regarding some issues was obtained after serious study and investigation, but the Association had not yet been able to assess the full scope of certain economic problems, for example. Third, there were only so many members and a limited budget to work with. Fourth, the Association had not yet obtained sufficient public recognition.

Given the fact that APJ wanted to develop as a solid,

balanced, three-pronged association, it made the strategic decision to stress thoroughness, comprehensiveness, and carefulness rather than rushing ahead with a shotgun approach and a full array of immature declarations, position papers, candidates for office, and political programs. It made no effort to put itself into the public light on false premises or with publicity gimmicks. Not only did this seem to be a more responsible way to develop, it was based on a realistic assessment of the American situation in which APJ found itself.

Political talk is cheap in the United States; there are hundreds of organizations—many good, many bad—claiming to be working for this or that cause. A small Christian organization will not accomplish much by a lot of superficial rhetoric, a flurry of proposals, and the attempt to do big things, most of which are already being done by some other organization. It must grow strong on the basis of a principled approach that demonstrates its quality and staying power to a growing number of citizens. The more solid and thorough its foundation in a community of Christian citizens, the more it should be able to accomplish in the long run.

A political association has a growth tempo of its own. It must lay a good foundation. It must not be too dependent on superficial signs of influence and power or on one personality or idea. It must broaden and deepen its grasp of political life year after year so that its record of achievement gradually emerges beyond question.

Thus APJ concluded very early that a political association must be able to learn what *not* to do as well as to decide what it *should* do at various stages in its development. It decided not to take positions too quickly on issues where it had no adequate basis in policy research. It decided to concentrate on gathering and developing a community of political talents built on a common Christian perspective as the basis for solid achievement in future years. It decided not to spend more money than it could obtain from committed members and supporters, so that it would not overextend itself in a debilitating or misleading way.

Some of these decisions, and others as well, are simply a reflection of good stewardship patterns in any organization. But they are especially important, it seems clear, in the development of a Christian political organization.

We have considered briefly five different kinds of consequences that have followed from a particular understanding of political life. Perhaps in the process of discussion, other consequences can be conceived and evaluated. A serious Christian political effort ought to be able to come to grips with the real situation in which those Christians find themselves, and an organized effort of the type that we have discussed should be able to demonstrate some unique insight and offer something special to the political community in which it functions.

Questions and Suggestions for Discussion

1. What are your impressions of the structure of authority described in the first part of this chapter? Do you think a political organization should have a different structure of authority? What kind of role should a local group or local chapter have within a larger national organization? What structure of authority should a local organization have?
2. Can you see any advantages in a Christian political association becoming a political party right at the beginning of its existence?
3. Take time as a group to discuss program options for a young political organization. For example, what would attract you to a Christian political association? What are the most important issues that such an organization ought to be studying? What are some things that a local group could do to learn about and contribute to a Christian political effort? What kinds of activities should a Christian political association engage in?

Additional Suggestions for Group Discussion

4. Do you see the reasoning behind APJ's support of a pluralistic school structure where the government does not own and control one of the school systems but attempts to do justice to a variety of schools? Can you see problems in such a system that might lead to injustice? For purposes of discussion, the group might want one of its members to study the APJ pamphlet "Justice for Education" and report on it in the group.
5. Do you understand how the system of proportional representation works? Do you know of countries where it exists? What problems do you think might arise within a system of proportional representation? Do you think those problems are more serious than the ones we now have within the present single-member district system?
6. Ask someone in the group, or perhaps a political scientist not in the group, to report on different systems of political representation in other countries, particularly those which have some form of proportional representation.
7. A key problem for any organization is raising funds. How do you think a Christian political association should go about raising funds sufficient for its program? How can it attract dues-paying members? How can it educate Christians about the need of Christian political service so that they will contribute to its work financially?
8. In this chapter, five main types of consequences have been discussed briefly. What other consequences do you think ought to come from a Christian political effort?

For Further Reading

Bob Goudzwaard, *Aid for the Overdeveloped West.*
Goudzwaard gives a number of examples of consequences that ought to flow from a Christian ap-

proach to political/economic affairs. His creative insight from a Christian perspective is very helpful, and a group might want to use his small book of relatively short essays for further discussion. See also the comments at the end of Chapter 1.

Goudzwaard, *A Christian Political Option.*
See the comments at the end of Chapter 4.

Mark O. Hatfield, *Between a Rock and a Hard Place* (Waco, Texas: Word Books, 1976).
Senator from Oregon, Mark Hatfield, goes into considerable depth in reflecting on political life from a Christian perspective in this book. Moreover, he shows how he has arrived at some conclusions about nuclear power, political and economic centralization, the deterioration of the environment, and the problem of world hunger during the course of his service in political life.

"Justice for Education," a pamphlet published by APJ.
A more detailed argument is developed in this pamphlet that explains the position summarized in the third section of this chapter.

"Justice for Representation," a pamphlet published by APJ.
See the comments at the end of Chapter 5.

Anthony King, editor, *The New American Political System* (Washington, D.C.: American Enterprise Institute, 1978).
A fine collection of essays by well-known political scientists and political commentators on the contemporary developments in almost every aspect of political life in the U.S.

Jeane Jordan Kirkpatrick, *Dismantling the Parties: Reflections on Party Reform and Party Decomposition* (Washington, D.C.: American Enterprise Institute, 1979).
An argument by a resident scholar at the American Enterprise Institute that the decomposition of the major political parties is due to efforts to reform

them. No consideration is given here to the possibility of a system of proportional representation as a means to strengthening the parties.

Rockne McCarthy, James Skillen, and William Harper, *Disestablishment a Second Time: Public Justice for American Schools* (forthcoming).

A detailed study of the historical, philosophical, legal, and political roots of the American system of education from the colonial period to contemporary Supreme Court decisions. The book concludes with a proposal for a pluralistic system of education. The volume is an outgrowth of research carried on by these members of the policy research group of the Association for Public Justice and the APJ Education Fund.

Hugh and Karmel McCullum and John Olthuis, *Moratorium: Justice, Energy, the North, and the Native People* (Toronto: Anglican Book Centre, 1977).

The outgrowth of work done by the Committee for Justice and Liberty in Canada, a Christian political association, along with other groups. It provides an excellent example of the consequences of a Christian political effort in regard to questions of energy, environment, and the plurality of cultural groups in Canada.

Douglas Rae, *The Political Consequences of Electoral Laws* (New Haven, Conn.: Yale University Press, 1971).

One of the best scholarly comparisons of a single-member district system and a proportional system of representation. Includes a good discussion of the advantages and disadvantages of both systems.

Peter Schouls, *Insight, Authority, and Power* (Toronto: Wedge Publishing Foundation, 1972).

A discussion of the nature of authority in different social offices, including the home, church, and school. The discussion here, from a Christian point of view, would be of help to a group concerned with the implications of biblical teaching for authority in a human organization.

7

Where Do We Go from Here?

Perhaps the most important point that should be made at the beginning of this final chapter is that political deeds pertain to the entire political community. That is to say, a small group or an individual interested in *doing* something about politics must take into account the real character of political life and understand what constitutes politically significant action.

For example, in view of the energy crisis, a small group might commit itself to obeying the speed limits and not using air conditioners. It also might decide to study the energy situation in depth and try to educate fellow citizens about the best policies for government to promote in order to conserve energy. All of these actions would be significant in themselves and should certainly be encouraged. But clearly the first ones mentioned are limited, personal responses that will not, in themselves, have any great political effect, though they are relatively easy to accomplish because each person can fulfill the commitment by an act of his or her own will. Moreover, although obeying the speed limit is an act of obedience to public law, the decision not to use an air conditioner is not, strictly speaking, a political act. The second set of actions is a different matter. The investigation and study of energy issues, even among members of a small group, will have to be coordinated. Due to the complexity of the problem, it may take months and years for a small group to come to a clear consensus on the basis of a thorough understanding of the matter. And there remains the task of educating and convincing fellow citizens of the best public policies. Depending on the size of the group doing the work, its efforts still might have no effect whatever on federal policy, though it might be able to influence local policy in a significant way.

The point is simply that the nature of politics must not be underestimated. There should be no illusion that this chapter can show a small group "how to" elect a President, or "how to" change America's political system. Nevertheless, if many people in many groups can learn how to do what is at hand for them to do, and at the same time can find a way to work together with all the others through a national organization, then it will be possible to see the connection between small deeds and big problems, between concerted efforts and great influence.

No substitute for understanding

For both the long and short runs, there is no substitute for understanding. The most underestimated political deed in the United States is political thinking. We have been so influenced by pragmatism in America that we have come to see government and politics as merely a process of fire-fighting—solving immediate problems within the framework of present assumptions and social structures. No serious thinking or critical evaluation is required of citizens about the system as a whole; all we need to do is act quickly to put out as many fires as possible. Our political attention span is shorter than a baby's. We respond to election campaigns of the moment; we gripe when taxes or inflation climb. But we do not think or act for the long run in a concerted, principled way because we tend to think that such deeds are useless for solving today's problems.

We should be reminded, however, that almost every

major characteristic of contemporary politics was at one time merely a new idea that did not fit into the political reality of that day. Slavery was once legitimate; democratic participation was once unthinkable; the idea of the rule of law was once an insult to kings; child labor was once acceptable; and we could go on and on. Changes came about because people's views of political life changed.

Now this is not to say that thinking is something in itself, something that can be carried on in a vacuum and then applied to political practice out of the blue. On the contrary, our political reflection must always be *engaged* reflection, always dealing with the full reality of political life. Nevertheless, there is no reason why we should not learn to evaluate that reality from a new perspective, to consider it from the vantage point of principles and presuppositions that are different from the ones that dominate the outlooks of other citizens.

The burden of this study guide has been that a different frame of reference for Christians should allow us to come to a *deeper* and *better* understanding of political life than is possible for those who do not take seriously a normative Christian view of politics. If that is so, then a new perspective on politics that captures a growing community of Christians can have a very significant effect on the shape of public policy and political processes in the long run.

Therefore, the first and most obvious deed that an individual or a small group can accomplish is to seek better understanding of political life from a Christian perspective. Here are some suggestions for steps that can be taken in that direction.

(1) Take a particular political issue that is of common interest to the members of your group. Pursue serious study and discussion of the issue toward the goal of trying to agree on what the problem really is and how it should be dealt with publicly in a just way. Let one person do some historical investigation; another pursue biblical study; another interview some public officials; another study the contemporary debates and options reported in the media and journals. As a group try to get beyond the confines of

the present discussion of the issue by analyzing the difference between Christian and non-Christian views of the matter.

(2) Take up a question about political life that is not so much a specific issue but a more general question about Christian principles, historical development, or biblical interpretation. Your group might want to gain a better understanding of the idea of "office," for example, or of the relationship between this age and the coming age, or of the compatability of Christianity and democracy, or any number of other general questions. These are legitimate political concerns, and while they should be studied with a view to their significance for contemporary political responsibility, they should not be ignored simply because they seem to be pragmatically less useful in the short run. Once again, divide the study responsibilities among the members. Invite in a guest or two—a biblical scholar, a political scientist, a historian, or someone else you know who can contribute to the debate and to your understanding.

(3) Your group might be more interested in coming to understand how the present system works. Isolate a particular dimension of the political system that interests you, perhaps the state or federal court system; the local city government; a particular branch of the state or federal bureaucracy; a legislator's office; or some other part. Do some good background reading; interview officials in that area; follow a court case, or a bill, or a policy decision, through all the channels of the structure that you are studying. And once again, do not stop at observation! Spend time discussing the good and bad features of what you are observing. Ask if something better could be done, and what it would take to change the system.

(4) Another option would be for your group to investigate carefully the process of civic education that is now carried on in and around your circles. Perhaps a local schoolteacher or principal could take an evening to explain how the elementary and secondary schools teach students about government, politics, and citizenship—showing

you the textbooks used and explaining the attitude that motivates the teaching process. Perhaps one or two members of the group could analyze two or three local and regional newspapers and national newsmagazines over several weeks or months. What are your churches doing? What instruction do they give, or what attitudes do they help to instill? What do the local, state and federal governments do to educate citizens? What do the parties do? Are there groups such as the League of Women Voters active in your area? After a careful assessment of all these dimensions of civic education, perhaps your group could try to come up with suggestions and criticisms that would improve what is now being done or that would inject something new into the process.

Whatever project you adopt, be sure to look for help in the suggestions for further reading at the end of each chapter.

Organizing events

A second general category of political deeds that both small and large groups can accomplish is that of organizing specific events. The activities suggested in the preceding section were longer-term study projects that a group can pursue primarily for the purpose of enlarging the political understanding of its members. The activities we will discuss in this section should also contribute to the growth of understanding, but most of them are single, specific events designed to reach or draw in people who are not necessarily part of a study group.

(1) The simplest type of event to organize would be closely connected with the ongoing work of a study group. At the point where such a group decides to invite in a guest speaker or to go out to interview a particular person, it could do a little extra work to make that occasion more of a public event. It does not have to be a big event to be worthwhile. The group could simply invite in a few extra friends for that evening. If the group happens to be associated with one or more churches, it might want to an-

nounce the event in the church bulletins, welcoming others for that particular occasion.

If the person being interviewed happens to be a public official or political figure, an announcement for the event might be placed in a local newspaper or included in some other circulars that reach a broader public. Perhaps your group has been studying urban housing development, or the state's income tax structure, or federal energy policy. At a certain juncture it becomes possible for you to speak with an official or expert on the matter. That is when you might arrange a very simple news conference, or a public forum, or an evening discussion with coffee where you would have the opportunity not only to do what you had already planned to do, but also to let a broader public in on the educational process and to introduce them to the work of your group.

(2) A second type of event would have some of the same goals as the first, but it would have more of a life and identity of its own. We are referring here to an evening lecture, a dinner meeting, a one-day conference, or something similar to one of these. The first type of occasion mentioned above would be successful even if no guests came, because the study group would have been able to fulfill its primary purpose for itself. But the second type is organized primarily for the benefit of a larger audience that would be assembled for the event, and therefore it has to be planned and advertised much more carefully to guarantee its success.

The details involved in organizing an event like this include: selecting an important, timely and interesting topic; preparing a realistic budget; finding an appropriate location; preparing refreshments or meals; obtaining the best speakers at a cost that is within reach of the group; arranging for publication display tables at the location of the event; advertising and promoting the event; taking care of special transportation needs (to and from airports or bus stations); and selecting the best master of ceremonies for the occasion. As you will discover, there are other details that will confront you later, if not sooner. In promoting the occasion, do not expect that printed advertisements in newspapers or bulletins will be enough. Personal contact is essential. Visiting friends, calling people by phone, meeting with other groups (large and small) to tell them about the meaning and purpose of the event are absolutely necessary.

The logistics of this type of event can simply be expanded to make possible a larger conference—something designed to last for more than one day and to include more people.

(3) A third type of event could be called a seminar or workshop. The purpose here is not so much to draw in a large audience for educational and inspirational purposes, but to deepen the understanding that some have of a particular issue, problem, or strategy for action.

If, for example, your group has concluded its work on U.S. agricultural policy or on the biblical idea of justice, it might want to test and refine its results by bringing together three or four "experts" for a day or two of serious discussion and debate. A seminar setting of this type should not be too large—perhaps 7 to 20 people. The material to be discussed should be placed in the hands of the participants well in advance of the seminar. Brief, concise summaries of the work should be presented at the beginning of the seminar by those who have done the work. Both friendly and not-so-friendly critics should be invited. Each one should be given plenty of time to present his or her assessment and critique. Someone from the organizing group should be prepared to take careful notes or to record the sessions on tape.

Another motivation for holding a seminar or workshop might be to deliver a "wrapped package" to a small group of leaders or trainees. Perhaps your group wants to prepare a small group of discussion leaders for their work at an upcoming conference. A half-day or one-day workshop might be the best way to get them all together and to train them for their tasks.

(4) A fourth type of event would be to organize the delivery of a specific political influence program. Perhaps

your group has come to some firm conclusions about city health policy. You decide that you want to deliver your conclusions to the city council or to the state's department of health. Or perhaps your concern is to try to help elect a candidate in the next federal or state election. Or perhaps your program plan is to help defend someone who is being taken to court. There are so many differences and peculiarities in each case that we cannot generalize easily about every possibility, but there are several things to keep in mind.

First, you should make sure that your plan fits in constructively with the larger program of the national organization to which you belong or with other groups that might be able to cooperate with you. Local groups in the Associations for Public Justice, for example, pursue programs of this sort as part of the entire Association's program. A small group might have far less influence and success than a larger one. But perhaps you are in an independent group of citizens acting on your own. In that case, make your first step an inquiry to see if there are others (perhaps APJ) that might be able to cooperate with you on this occasion for a specific purpose.

Second, you should make every effort to assess the requirements and costs of your plan at the outset. Taking one day for three of you to drive to the state capitol to deliver the message is one thing. Taking weeks to gather signatures for a petition, or to attend a series of city council meetings, or to follow a case through the courts is something quite different. Starting a program that you cannot finish will not only be a failure, it could also discourage you from any further action.

Finally, this kind of specific action, oriented toward a particular goal, should never be approached simply for itself. Whether you are successful or unsuccessful in reaching your goal, the conclusion of the event should not bring about the end of your existence or activities as a group. Each event or program should be approached as part of the ongoing responsibility that you have as Christian citizens. The event should not become the tail that wags the dog.

Formulating proposals

A third category of political activities includes drawing up policy options and program proposals. Here are some suggestions.

(1) If your group has been working on a particular issue or group of related issues and you have come to some conclusions about your town's need for better park facilities, or about your state's laws governing the adoption of children, or about the federal government's farm policy, then you might be ready to embark on a project of actually formulating a policy for the government. Even if you do not believe that you are professionally qualified to draw up such a proposal, the exercise of doing so, and of finding out how public policy is made, might be a very worthwhile action.

Once again it is not easy to generalize about all the possibilities, but at the very least you will want to make sure that you do some of the following:

a) Gather all the helpful advice and good information on the subject that you can. In other words, you must do your homework carefully.
b) Hold a seminar or workshop of some sort (as suggested in the last section) in which you receive serious evaluation of your work.
c) Consult with policy makers who can give you details about the form in which your policy should be drawn up.
d) Investigate the means of delivering your proposal to those who should have it, including government officials, party leaders, and the media.

(2) Not only do governments at all levels need policies, but organizations such as the Association for Public Justice need both public policy options as well as proposals for their own programs. Perhaps before proceeding with your action in number 1 above, you could send a copy of your project plan to the national office of several organizations to ask if the work of your group could be supported by (or at least useful to) those organizations. Or if, as an in-

dependent group, you have completed a policy proposal, you might consider sending it to one or more political associations as a stimulus for their work and in the hope of winning their support.

Perhaps your interest as a group is not in public policy formulation but in developing a program proposal for other groups similar to your own or for a national association. If you have discovered a particularly successful way to organize a conference, or to distribute information to citizens, or to conduct the work of a study group, or to organize a community supper, or to influence public opinion, or any number of other things, why not take as your project the writing up of that program as a recommendation to others? You might want to put it in the form of an article for a Christian magazine, or put it together with several proposals into a small book, or distribute it through other means. The point is that after someone has developed a new food preparation, it is sometimes legitimate to share the recipe. It is certainly one of APJ's aims to foster this kind of creativity and sharing, and to serve as a clearing house for such program recommendations.

(3) A final suggestion under this category is a variation on the first two. Whether you are interested in public policy or in the programs of a voluntary political association, it is almost certain that your specific concern will be of interest to other institutions or organizations. For example, the political science department of a nearby college or university might be interested in having one of its students or professors cooperate in your project aimed at influencing electoral apathy in local and state elections. A local church or group of churches might be interested in cooperating on a project that deals with the causes of poverty. Local schools, a labor union local, a business enterprise, or several families might be willing to cooperate with your group in formulating a policy or developing a program proposal that vitally affects them.

Before initiating your project, then, you might want to take a little time to inquire about whether your project on housing policy would receive the support of some families or of the college sociology department; or whether your project on local and state tax rates would be supported by a local business or labor union; or whether your project of writing down your successful experience in sponsoring workshops would be of interest to some churches or APJ.

Strategies, tactics, causes, and coalitions

Political life is like most other dimensions of human life in that it requires decisions from responsible people in the middle of circumstances and situations which can never be fully anticipated or prepared for. It is not possible at this point, for example, to say what specific strategies and tactics will be necessary for you or for a national political association a year from now. But just as each citizen must decide month by month and year by year how to fulfill his or her political responsibilities, so Christians together must decide what should be done inside and outside of political organizations.

There are four general categories of decisions that face a Christian political association, and they also face each Christian and each group of Christians in public life. In looking briefly at these four categories, it will be possible to focus in yet another way on the question: Where do we go from here?

(1) A strategy is a long-range plan or program developed to achieve certain ends. An individual citizen might decide, for example, to follow a strategy of cooperating with others or of remaining alone in trying to fulfill his or her civic responsibilities. We have already discussed, in Chapter 5, elements of the general strategy that APJ is following in its development. Part of APJ's strategy is to recognize that individual Christians and groups of Christians will need to develop strategies of their own at different times and places when and where it is impossible for APJ to serve them adequately. At the same time, the Association hopes to find ways to encourage such individuals and groups to bring their insights and contributions into the

strategic development of APJ so that it can grow stronger in carrying out its strategies as an organization. As individuals, and as a discussion group, you should be asking yourselves what strategies you will be adopting to fulfill your civic responsibilities.

(2) The word "tactic" is sometimes used to mean the same thing as "strategy." But it is also used to indicate a more specific or limited device or plan that is employed within a larger strategy. Here we might say, for example, that if the Association for Public Justice wants to accomplish its strategy of developing a three-pronged structure and program, it will have to make dozens of tactical decisions about how to build a larger membership, how to nurture more and better research associates, how to raise money, how to get its point across to members of Congress, and a host of others. Once again, you and your group should be asking yourselves about the tactics you should use in contemporary public life.

(3) Causes are the specific political battles that must be fought. APJ hopes to be of service to Christians by helping to sort out the more important from the less important causes that should be handled. Questions that citizens must ask and answer include the following. Are the causes which preoccupy most people today the really important ones? If so, how should Christians attack them? If not, what should be done? If there are more causes to deal with than time or money allows, which ones should be left alone and which ones picked up? You and your group might spend some time asking about the causes that most concern you, and about which strategies and tactics you think will be necessary to deal with those causes.

(4) Finally, there is the crucial question of coalitions. How should different Christian associations work together when they disagree about specific issues? How should Christian and non-Christian organizations work together, especially when they agree about what should be done in certain situations? How long-lasting should a political coalition be? How do different partners in a coalition maintain their own identities? Most political work requires

cooperation among different groups and organizations for the achievement of specific goals. Building coalitions is a regular part of political life. APJ must make decisions about cooperative efforts inside and outside coalitions. So must you.

The future of justice in America is dependent, in part, on the response of Christians to God's Word which calls them to serve Him and their neighbors according to His norm of justice. Those of us claiming to be Christians must heed His call, and we may do so because of what He has already done for us in Christ Jesus, the Lord, the Righteous One, the just Judge, the King, our Savior. Where do we go from here? We ought to follow Jesus, and that means rendering careful public service in our own historical situation for the establishment of public justice.

Questions and Suggestions for Discussion

1. Having concluded the reading and discussion connected with this study guide, take some time as a group to assess the value of your work together. Try to answer some of the following questions:
   a) Are there some things that almost all of you agree were very valuable about your study together? What were they?
   b) What are the most troublesome or perplexing questions that remain for you?
   c) Are there any basic disagreements among you that are still unresolved?
   d) If you could subtract from, add to, or change this book in any way, what would you do?
2. Are you at the point now where you would consider taking up one of the projects suggested in this chapter? If so, why, and what do you think you would like to do? If not, why not?
3. For purposes of concluding your group discussion (perhaps in the final session together), have each member take a different chapter and comment briefly on

what that chapter contributed to his or her understanding and to the group's understanding.

4. If some or all of the members of the group are interested in pursuing further discussion together, spend part of a session discussing other books and materials that you might want to study next.

Additional Suggestions for Group Discussion

5. Take an issue or problem of political life that is very alive in the public mind at this moment and discuss it with the purpose of trying to decide how your use of this study guide has made a difference in helping you to evaluate that problem or issue.
6. Where else might this study guide prove useful beyond the group in which you have just used it? In a Sunday school class in church? In a Bible study group? In a college or high school classroom? In a family?
7. If more people are going to gain a Christian understanding of political life and begin working together in politics, what are the three or four steps that must be taken from here, in your estimation? Which of those steps would your group be willing and able to take?

For Further Reading

And He Had Compassion on Them: The Christian and World Hunger (Grand Rapids: Christian Reformed Board of Publications, 1978), and *For My Neighbor's Good* (same publisher, 1979).

Two excellent books for study purposes that take up the issue of world hunger and show how that problem is related to Christian responsibility. Since they are designed as study guides, a group might want to consider using one or both of them in a future program of discussion.

Kenneth M. Dolbeare, *Political Change in the United States* (New York: McGraw-Hill, 1974).

Though Dolbeare's book is not written from a Christian perspective, it offers many insights into the nature of political action and political change, and it is especially helpful in showing how consciousness and understanding must change if political change is to take place.

John W. Gardner, *In Common Cause: Citizen Action and How It Works* (New York: W.W. Norton, 1973).

Gardner is the founder of the citizens' organization "Common Cause." Although the view of political action is different from that of this study guide, the book shows how one citizens' organization works.

Barbara Ward, *Five Ideas That Changed the World: Nationalism, Industrialism, Colonialism, Communism, Internationalism* (New York: W. W. Norton, 1959).

A group looking for a book that will introduce them to some of the main political ideologies of our day should consider using this small, interesting, paperback book by a leading political thinker. Each chapter introduces one of the five ideas.

Albert Wolters, "Ideas Have Legs," in Ed Vanderkloet, editor, *A Christian Union in Labour's Wasteland* (see Chapter 5).

Wolters's article helps to show the way that "ideas" guide and influence actions. Written from a Christian perspective, it is very helpful in enlarging on the points made at the beginning of this chapter.

Some of the books to which you might want to return for group discussion purposes include the following: Egbert Schuurman, *Reflections on the Technological Society* (see Chapter 1); E. F. Schumacher, *Small is Beautiful* (see Chapter 1); and Richard Mouw, *Politics and the Biblical Drama* (see Chapter 2).

Some of the publications introduced earlier that might prove helpful for those interested in formulating proposals are: Bob Goudzwaard, *Aid for the Overdeveloped West* (see Chapter 1); Ronald Sider, *Rich Christians in an Age of Hunger* (see Chapter 1); Arthur Simon, *Bread for the World* (see Chapter 1); APJ's "Justice for Education" (see Chapter 6); and Hugh and Karmel McCullum and John Olthuis, *Moratorium* (see Chapter 6).

Appendix

Constitutional Affirmations of the Association for Public Justice

Preamble

As Christian citizens we join with the Psalmist in a song of thanksgiving to the Lord.

> Sing to the Lord, all the earth;
> Sing to the Lord, bless His name;
> Proclaim good tidings of His salvation from day to day.
>
> Say among the nations, "The Lord reigns;
> Indeed, the world is firmly established, it will not be moved;
> He will judge the peoples with equity."
> [The Lord] is coming to judge the earth.
> He will judge the world in righteousness,
> And the peoples in His faithfulness (Psalm 96:1-2, 10, 13).

Called together by the good tidings of the Lord's grace and mercy, we humbly acknowledge our responsibility for many of the injustices in the United States and in the relationships between the United States and countries around the world. We confess that to place ultimate trust in "the people" as the source of both political authority and constitutional sovereignty is an idolatrous faith. This truth has led our nation both domestically and internationally to impose the will of some "people" on others in ways that have often confused the power of majorities or of minorities with the power of justice, thereby encouraging arrogance, greed, materialism, racism, sexism, oppression of the weak and the poor, and countless other forms of injustice.

We pray that, in face of so many national and international injustices, God, through Christ Jesus, will graciously forgive us our complicity in political unrighteousness and give us insight and courage so that (1) we may understand the positive political significance of the great commandments to love God fully and our neighbors as ourselves, and that (2) we may exercise the kind of political service that will encourage the establishment of justice and aid the restraint of injustice so that all peoples might enjoy an increasing measure of God's joyful and peaceful purpose for human life on earth.

With thanksgiving, confession of sin, and prayerful expectation before the Lord we join in organizing this association.

Article I — Name

The name of the organization shall be the Association for Public Justice.

Article II — Objects

This association endeavors to foster all those activities which promote the understanding and achievement of public justice.

Article III — Basis

By the authority of the Scriptures of the Old and New Testaments we confess that God through Jesus Christ has chosen to vindicate His will to establish justice in the creation. Through Christ's obedience to His Father's will, including His atoning death on the cross, He fulfills God's plan to establish righteousness in the world. The Father sent His Son to us as the light of the world—the light which also illumines our political path. In His light we are able to understand our calling to be obedient to Him as servants and disciples. We believe that God's Word exposes our sin and guilt, teaches us that all of human life should unfold as service to God, and draws us together through His grace into a new life of political responsibility. Accordingly, through faith in Christ, in the power of His resurrection, we hereby commit ourselves to live politically in keeping with the following affirmations. We believe

1. that any establishment of justice in the world is possible only because of God's judgment and redemption of the creation in Jesus Christ who, as King of kings, possesses all authority in heaven and on earth. Out of the power of His resurrection all authority on earth is delegated by Him as a responsible stewardship. He delegates this authority directly to institutions such as families, schools, churches, and the state.

2. that the state should have its specific identity as a territorial legal community of public justice. "Public Justice" indicates the normative calling of the state whose legitimate functions are established internally by public legal principles and limited externally by the task which God delegates directly to other social institutions. The proper task of the state is to bind together, in a public legal community, all persons, groups, and institutions within its territory.

3. that government is the office of human authority within the political community (state) which is called

by God to establish, enforce, and adjudicate laws for the sake of public justice, and that citizens of the state may, through elected representatives with a free mandate, legitimately exercise influence in legislation and in the general direction of the policies of their government.

4. that the principles of public justice demand of government an equitable handling of the goods, services, welfare, protection, and opportunity that it controls, without penalty or special advantage to any person, organization, institution or community due to religious, racial, linguistic, sexual, economic or other social and individual differences.

5. that the policies of government should be founded on the recognition that the ongoing development of human culture can thrive only in responsible freedom. Government therefore has no authority to direct society by attempting to gain control of the internal life of non-political communities, institutions, and organizations. Rather, it should restrict itself, in accord with the principles of public justice, to encouraging, protecting, and making room for the development of the full range of cultural life, giving special attention to those minority groups or aspects of human culture which may from time to time be oppressed or in danger of losing their freedom to develop.

6. that no person or community of persons anywhere ought to be compelled by governmental power to subscribe to this or any other political creed, and that the government of any state ought to honor the conscientious objections that any of its citizens may have against a governmentally imposed obligation, provided these objections do not conflict with the demands of public justice.

Also by the APJ Education Fund:

Confessing Christ and Doing Politics, ed. James W. Skillen, essays by Senator Mark Hatfield, Joel Nederhood, Rockne McCarthy, Gordon Spykman, Bernard Zylstra, and the editor.
ISBN: 0-936456-02-7